Georgia Bonesteel's

Patchwork Potpourri

Georgia Bonesteel's Patchwork Potpourri

The University of North Carolina Press Chapel Hill and London

To

Jinkinson Payne

and

Anna Frances,

the next generation

of creative hands

© 1997 Georgia Bonesteel

All rights reserved

Manufactured in the United States of America

Ruler designs Copyright 1986, 1995, OMNIGRID®, Inc. All rights reserved. U.S. Pat. 4,779,346; Ca. Pat. 1,297,286

The paper in this book meets the guidelines for permanence and durability of the Committee on Production Guidelines for Book Longevity of the Council on Library Resources.

Library of Congress Cataloging-in-Publication Data

Bonesteel, Georgia.

[Patchwork potpourri]

Georgia Bonesteel's patchwork potpourri.

p.   cm.

Includes index.

ISBN 0-8078-4660-0 (pbk.: alk. paper)

1. Patchwork — Patterns.   2. Quilting.

3. Appliqué.   I. Title.

TT835.B6123   1997

746.46'041 — dc21   96-52460

CIP

01   00   99   98   97   5   4   3   2   1

Contents

Introduction

Where have the years gone? They say when you are having fun, time flies. I guess that explains my patchwork life. So many quilts, so many students, so many travels, so many stitches, so much fabric, and so little time. Each class and every mistake, each trip and every new piece of fabric, has presented me with new opportunities. It has been my privilege and pleasure to teach quilting for twenty-five years; yet when asked what my profession is, I always answer, "professional quiltmaker." However, what I really mean is "quiltmaking promoter," since I advocate quilting as a creative outlet that rewards you in the end with not only a wonderful product but a feeling of true accomplishment. For many of us, it's difficult to believe everyone has not joined our bandwagon. Those who do not sew are just missing out on a lot of fun.

Why do we quilt? Sometimes I wonder. What possesses us to drive miles out of our way to investigate a new fabric shop? Why do grown women cry before a quilt that has won the blue ribbon? Who else spends countless hours planning, cutting, accepting, and rejecting small bits of fabric? I have concluded it's for one main reason: control! We might not be able to control taxes, the dentist bill, or the price of ground beef, but in our little world we can control the pattern, the fabric, the thread, the size, and most important, how soon we want to finish. Then, when we get all done, we have something to show for our efforts. If we are not completely satisfied, we can make it again in another color. Enjoy the process. Yes, as quilters we get frustrated sometimes, because it does take time to connect those three layers by hand, and it can be even more challenging to do it by machine. But look what we have when it's completed. That must be why we respect those blue ribbons at quilt shows. We know the energy and thought that go into every stitch.

The incentives for making a quilt are as varied as all the fabric that's ever been printed. To suggest that it's to keep warm doesn't begin to touch on the really serious motivation. Planning and executing every step along the way becomes the real challenge. Only you determine the outcome. This sense of self-satisfaction is best displayed at our quilt shows. The culmination of years of stitching is truly glorified on display for all to see. I have seen people's self-confidence and egos boosted and fulfilled at such events.

Your time is important. A teacher or an author steals that most precious product and asks that you respond. Now you must ask yourself why you quilt. Is it the legacy that you wish to pass on in your family? Is it the camaraderie experienced with friends and fellow guild members? Maybe it's the productive end that results in much gratification. Just imagine all the thoughts provoked while the needle moves up and down, or the solace that comes from simply holding the cloth. There are many benefits in a long mechanical task that requires a minimum of attention with soothing repetitious action. For all the fast, easy, quick, and cheap "buzz" words introduced into our quilt craft today, I do not think we should be fooled. It takes time, energy, and money. Yes, that's right, "A task easily done leaves little satisfaction." Join me and the many quiltmakers today to experience the joy of creating with fabric. Make a quilt!

My approach to quilting has changed over the years. I used to be filled with guilt if projects did not get done. The more I learned, the more unfinished objects accumulated on my shelves. Then one day I went to an exhibit of Monet's London Bridge paintings. It dawned on me that Monet worked on different canvases to correspond to various times of the day. As the light changed, he moved to another setting. My mother has told me that we are related to Claude Monet—many genes back—so I now feel quite justified jumping from one project to the next. I practice this Monet Method of gradually finishing my projects, never bored by the same color or pattern for too long. My sewing time is my production period at the sewing machine, and my quiet, quilting time is in the evening.

As I assembled this book and developed my new series on lap quilting for PBS television, I determined that I had a little bit of this and a lot of that—a mixed bag, of sorts. It soon became a potpourri of patchwork that includes techniques newly acquired, "tried and true" tips gathered over many years, "quilt math" developed for quick methods, and creative appliqué procedures. Because so much of our quilt enjoyment is shared, I have developed several projects that come under the heading Groupie Guidelines, where you can challenge one another to complete something together. I quite often like to come in the back door of patchwork; that is, instead of designing a block for a quilt and then choosing the fabric, why not let the fabric dictate the design of the block? That occurs in the Percolator Patchwork quilt, a picturelike design. What better reason to quilt than for a loved one? Holiday presents made from patchwork can be a yearlong endeavor or a jiffy baby quilt that comes in an oversized tote-all.

Choose a favorite project to make geared to your sewing level—beginner, intermediate, or advanced. I would never expect you to make every quilt in this book, but pick a favorite. Mine is the Seminole Skies. Seminole piecework takes on a new character when turned into mountains. This design did not come easy. I struggled with wrong cuts and colors before I finally got it right. It takes advantage of new angles and combines some familiar techniques, yet pushes one to explore many new possibilities—perhaps a beach scene with sand dune colors, or a mirror image with a lake in between. Join me, step by step, as I give you a choice of three sizes for this wall hanging.

The benefits of working with gridded freezer paper become more clear with each page of *Patchwork Potpourri*. It's inexpensive and can be reused many times. I like the control it gives me for cutting and sewing. If you have been searching for that perfect scrap quilt that also highlights your quilting lines, then spend time with the Corn and Beans Quilt. Wouldn't our grandmothers be surprised to see how far we have gone stitching through paper to make designs! Try stitching wildflower diamonds via paper patterns.

I trust you will gain some new ideas from reading my tips and hints. Keeping an open-door policy to changes and fabric opportunities allows us to grow. I treasure an old letter that came my way from Kentucky; it was written in 1931. The quilter is so proud of her feather quilting designs made with her tiny needles and the fact that her quilts are always so clean. She concludes her letter by saying, "I hope we are beginning a work that will last and that others may see my work and it may spread from one to another." Certainly that has been the role of all quilting teachers—spreading the good quilt word. So often, students underestimate their own powers. With gentle coaxing, encouragement, learning from mistakes, and perseverance, students soon exclaim, "Look, I did it myself!" Those are magic words for a teacher.

There is a resource index for products featured on my latest 900 series, produced by the University of North Carolina Center for Public Television. I always feel that the quilts come to life when I can come into your home via the television screen to unfurl each one. Your attention when you tune in to our shows is appreciated.

Thank you for buying this book. Good luck with all of your patchwork endeavors. Support your local public television station, your local quilt guild, and that cherished hometown landmark—your quilt shop full of fabric and "goodies." Thank heavens for yesterday's and today's quiltmakers.

Georgia Bonesteel's Patchwork Potpourri

1 Starting Out

The technique, "how-to" part of patchwork today is dependent on rotary cutters, thick rulers, and cutting mats. It's not unfair to say this has revolutionized our craft life in many ways. In fact, I sometimes feel sorry for scissors! Except for appliqué, they have taken a back seat to round rotary cutters. When you mix these tools with a calculator that includes some simple quilt math, you have a great combination. Examine each of these—quilt math, rulers, cutters, and mats—in your quilt life. Just how can you put them to best use and stay in the quilt mainstream?

The most repeated shapes in patchwork are the square, the rectangle, and the triangle. Each of these can be cut in cloth with a rotary cutter, including the seam allowance once the amount of additional fabric is calculated. Often more than one shape is needed, so we use a calculator to add and multiply for repeats of the same shape.

MATH QUILT FACTS

I developed a chart I call Math Quilt Facts, which you can tape to your calculator (fig. 1.1). Use a copy machine to reproduce this rectangular cutout and tape it to the backside of your calculator. It's a great way to learn the decimal system and to have the key to patchwork addition at your fingertips. If only I had learned math and geometry with fabric and a sewing machine. I have such a respect now for the exactness of numbers. The cloth has a life—it gives and bends—but numbers always stay the same. They can be relied on for trueness!

Learning to use my calculator has given me more quilting confidence and assurance. I hope you will take these math tips to heart. They are also a great way to check templates in a book!

MATH QUILT FACTS				
1/8" = .125		For	Add	To
1/4" = .25	□	.5	(1/2")	Height & Width
3/8" = .375	▭	.5	(1/2")	Height & Width
1/2" = .5	◺	.875	(7/8")	Height & Width
5/8" = .625	△	1.25	(1 1/4")	Base Width
3/4" = .75	△	.75	(3/4")	Each Side
7/8" = .875	Right Angle x 1.414 = Diagonal			
	Diagonal x .707 = Right Angle			

Binding Amount
Perimeter x bias width (2.5) = Area
√ Area + 2"= Required size of square

Figure 1.1

Let's look at some examples with repeated shapes, knowing that the seam allowance addition for patchwork is 1/4" (.25").

Squares

For any size of multiple cut squares, cut strips ½" (.5") wider than finished square size; then cut squares from the strips (fig. 1.2).

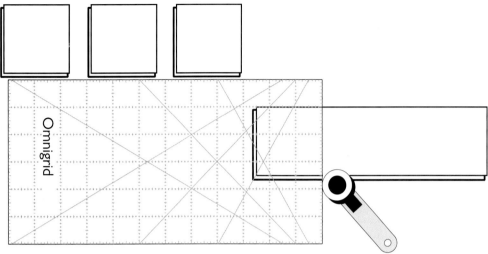

Figure 1.2

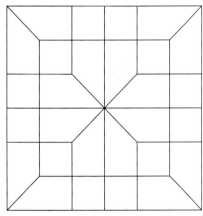

Figure 1.3

Sometimes, if a square is part of a given block, you have to decide the equal division of the square to determine the size. For example: Decide on the equal division of the block as in this four patch and then figure the equal division of each quarter section (fig. 1.3). To decide the size of cut squares, divide the quarter section by 3 on the calculator each time:

For a 6" block, 3" divided by 3 = 1" + .5" = 1.5".
For a 12" block, 6" divided by 3 = 2" + .5" = 2.5".
For a 14" block, 7" divided by 3 = 2.33" (almost 2.375") + .5"= 2.875".
For a 16" block, 8" divided by 3 = 2.666" (close to 2.625") + .5" = 3.125".

I have discovered a good technique for cutting squares of any size, using a square ruler. These rulers come in several sizes and have different numbers on each corner. If you are right-handed, place the corner of the ruler with the 1"–1" near the end in the upper right-hand corner on top of the fabric, covering the full amount of the area you need to cut. With a rotary cutter, cut the fabric square on the right side and on top of the ruler (see fig. 1.4a). Next, turn the ruler to the opposite corner, aligning the ruler lines exactly on the desired cut fabric square. Then cut the left side and the bottom side (fig. 1.4b). Here is your chance to use the opposite hand to cut, OR move to the other side of the table, OR turn the cutting mat, OR mark the lines with a chalk ruler, slide the ruler, and then cut on the exact lines. "Lefties" would start with the 1"–1" corner of the ruler in the upper left-hand position; cut left side and top; reverse to the opposite corner and proceed.

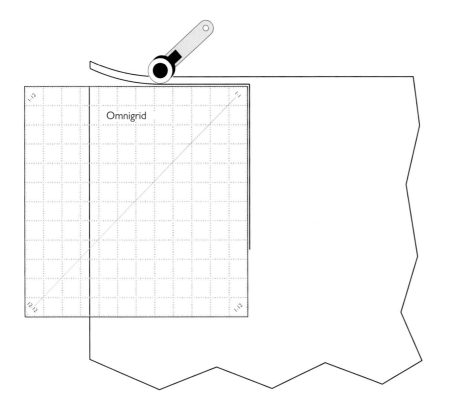

Figure 1.4a

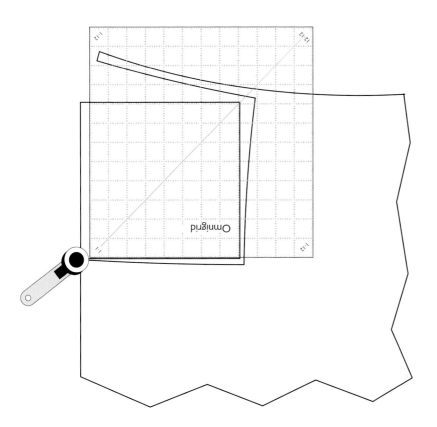

Figure 1.4b

Rectangles

To cut rectangles, start with the finished size and add ½" (.5") to the width and height for the cutout cloth size. For any long rectangles, turn the ruler the long way (fig. 1.5).

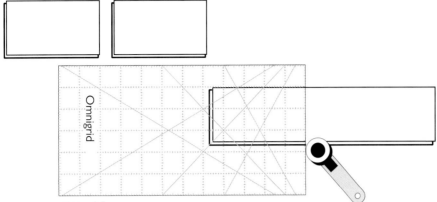

Figure 1.5

Triangles

To cut multiple triangles, add ⅞" (.875") to the right-angle height. This includes the diagonal point, which when sewn, is snipped off. I call them dog ears. This is achieved in quick-cutting long strips the desired width, then cutting the strips into squares, and then making one diagonal cut through each square (fig. 1.6).

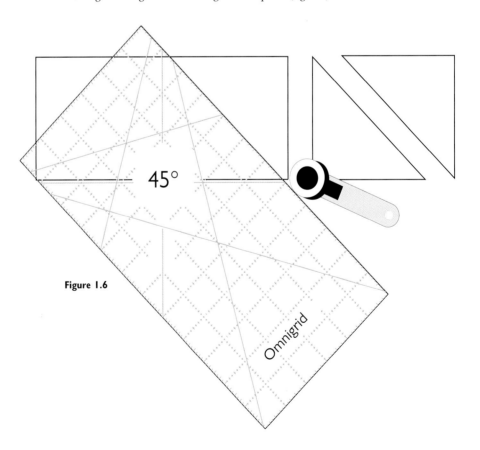

Figure 1.6

Half-Square Triangles

To make half-square (right-angle) triangles, use the same addition, but machine stitch a quarter-inch seam on each side of the diagonal line and then cut apart. Use a pencil or chalk roller, not a ballpoint pen, for this drawn line. Not only is this quick, but I especially like that the edges of the diagonal cut are so precise—no more "eeking" over the edge of one color (fig. 1.7).

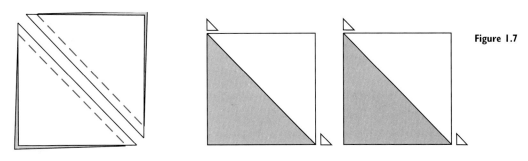

Figure 1.7

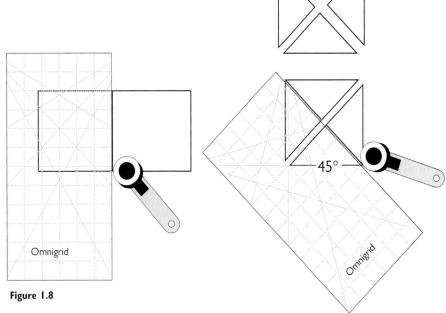

Pyramid Triangles

I put these in the same category since the long sides of these triangles are on the straight of the grain. Learn the distinction between the right-angle triangle and the pyramid triangle and you will never have to deal with bias edge blocks again. To cut out these repeated triangles, add 1¼" (1.25") to any strip of fabric. Then cut on the diagonal each way through the repeated cut squares (fig. 1.8).

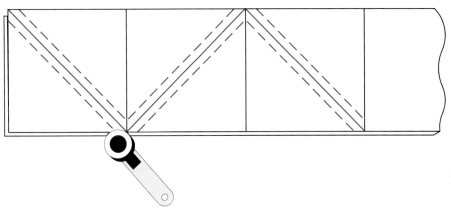

Figure 1.8

Quarter-Square Triangles

Stitch the same diagonal lines as the half-square triangles, but start with the 1¼" (1.25") addition. Cut apart each square on the diagonal; press closed seams toward the same fabric; trim dog ears and realign these half-square triangles with right sides together of contrasting fabrics. Draw another diagonal line, stitch on either side, and cut apart for quarter-square triangle sets. Be certain to release the seams at the intersection on the backside so all seams go in a concentric direction — release just the original ¼" stitches, not the connecting seam. This makes for a soft, well-balanced intersection (fig. 1.9).

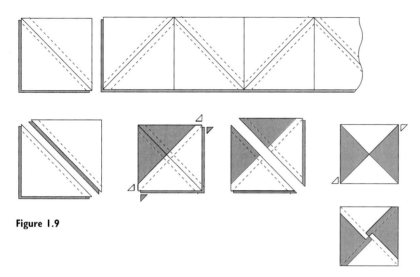

Figure 1.9

Equilateral Triangles

Add ¾" (.75") to the finished height (from base to point). This allows you to stack strips of fabric and cut out many scrap triangles with the seam allowance included on all three sides. Here the 60° angle on your ruler is the key angle for accurate repeat cutting (fig. 1.10).

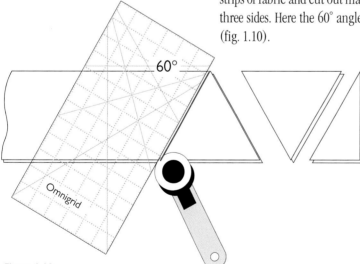

Figure 1.10

Key Measurements

To calculate the diagonal of any block, simply multiply the right angle by 1.414. To calculate the right angle of a block, simply multiply the diagonal by .707. Think of the times this can be used in quiltmaking: placing blocks on point across a bed, adding borders onto a block, or adding triangles onto a block to create a square within a square.

Binding Amount

Whether you cut the binding for a quilt on the straight of the grain or the bias, as in a bias tube, this formula works to yield the amount of fabric required. This will assist in purchasing fabric, especially if you want your quilt bound in the same fabric as the backing. Follow these steps:

1. Calculate the perimeter, the outside measurement of all sides.

2. Multiply that figure times the desired width of the binding. A standard cut is 2½". This gives enough width to fold the binding, aligning the raw edges of the quilt top and the binding; stitch to the quilt with a ¼" seam and roll this fold to the backside where the fold can be hand secured over the previous machine stitching. With this figure in place on the calculator, push the square root symbol of your calculator to reveal the size square required. I add 2" to that amount for quilter's insurance, to be certain I have enough, in case of a mistake.

Perimeter (outside measurement of all sides) × bias width or straight of grain (2½" [2.5"]) = area.

Square root of area = size square plus a quilter's insurance of 2".

TOOLS FOR CUTTING

Rulers

Thick, clear plastic rulers that are well marked with ⅛" markings and diagonal 45°, 30°, and 60° angles (see Omnigrid® products in fig. 1.11) are staples in our workrooms today. Along with a yardstick beam compass, I suggest the following starter set:

1" × 12"
6" × 6"
3" × 18"
6" × 12"
6" × 24"
12½" or 15" square
Triangles with built-in seam allowance (#96 and #98)

Rotary Cutters

They come in many brands and many sizes. I prefer cutters where I can see the blade move and where I can control the release of the blade. If you invest in a trio of sizes, you will use each one for different reasons. They are awkward to use at first, but once you gain confidence with the rotary cutters, they become indispensable.

The small one is for miniatures, cutting a single layer precisely, and executing curves.

The medium-sized cutter is an all-round versatile cutter, is the most popular, and will cut four layers perfectly.

The large cutter can handle six layers nicely, adapts to arthritic problems, and allows a lot of control. Once you start using this size, you will get "hooked."

Tips for Cutting Fabric

- **If two contrasting fabrics are to be sewn together, press and cut them out together with the right sides facing. That way you do not have to align raw edges before stitching. (I call it getting married—they have to go together for awhile!)**
- **Spray sizing on prewashed fabric to give it stability for cutting and stitching.**
- **Mark off any long straight of the grain borders to be cut before starting on the small strip cuts. I use a chalk roller for this.**
- **Never change rulers or cutters in the middle of a cutting project. Stick to the same tools for the entire project.**
- **Keep the full length of a big piece of fabric on the cutting area. Do not let excess fabric hang down, or your cut pieces will be distorted.**
- **Stand up when using a rotary cutter for the best "push pressure"; always cut away from yourself.**
- **Learn how to replace the blades; store your cutters in an old eyeglass case.**
- **Let the outside fingers of the off-hand fall off the ruler and grip the mat. Remember you have to bear down and apply pressure for the round cutter to work. Learn to cut with the opposite hand, which takes a lot of practice.**
- **Try not to lend your cutter to anyone.**

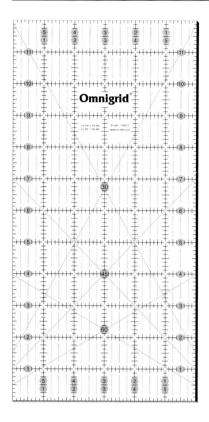

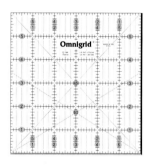

Figure 1.11

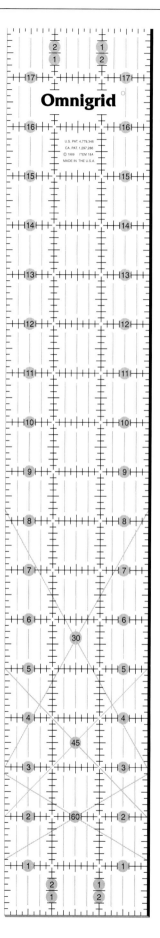

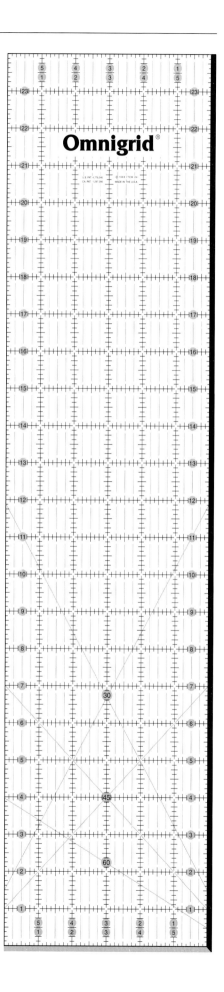

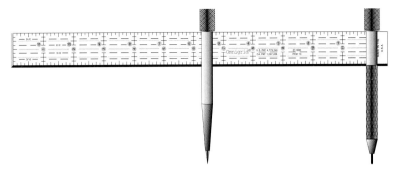

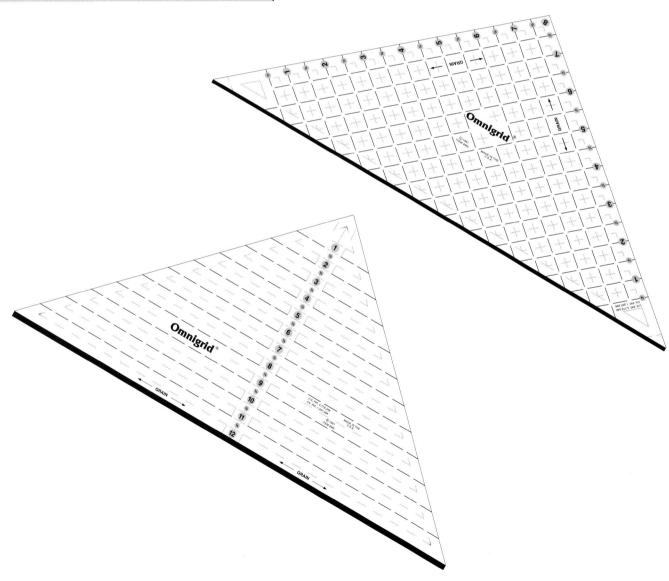

Mats

If you have a large cutting table, a full-size mat is a luxury and will spoil you forever. Traveling quilters who attend workshops should carry a medium-sized mat to fit into their "goody" bag. A cutting mat near your sewing machine is an asset for miniatures and paper piecing. Keep your mat out of direct sunlight, especially on a car seat!

TOOLS FOR QUILTING

Acquiring the necessary quilting tools depends on your goals. You do not have to own all these tools at one time—that takes time and money—but there are wonderful tools to accompany our mats, rulers, and cutters. We use these around the clock, so starting at 1:00 I have listed some of the most popular quilting tools that are referred to in *Patchwork Potpourri*.

Flexicurve: a curved drafting tool, 18" length preferred

Quilt stencil with marking tools: hera, pencils (for paper and cloth), chalk roller, and eraser

Hoops for machine quilting: 9" and 6"

Calculator and Math Facts card

Masking tape in various widths, down to ¼" (store in plastic bag)

Fabric with good quality thread— neutral colors plus metallics [at 6:00]

Needles: appliqué and hand quilting in various sizes

Pins

Glue stick: handy for appliqué and foundation piecing

Grid Grip®: gridded freezer paper and plastic template material

Seam ripper and a stiletto

Bias bars for making continuous bias strips

Scissors: paper, cloth, snippers, and appliqué lip

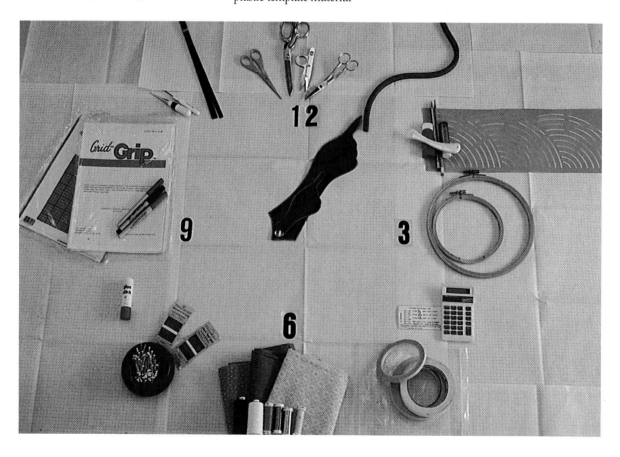

TECHNIQUE: FOLDED FLYING GEESE

A new, dimensional Folded Flying Geese technique produces a raised triangle. The formula for any size Flying Geese complex is the following: Cut two background squares or sections the desired height plus ½" (.5"). Cut a rectangle based on the finished height. Add ½" (.5") for one side and add ½" (.5") to the doubled height measurement. This is a great accent for vests, treetops, decorative collars, and novelty projects.

PROJECT: AMERICANA COLLAR

Make a decorative collar with pockets on each end of the long front ties. Finished size is 28" long, including a back panel 10" × 17".

Materials
1 yard of background fabric
1 yard of backing (Make 4 yards of continuous bias cut 2" wide for binding around the collar.) An optional finishing would not use binding, but a simple inverting using the lining (often called the "pillow-turned" method).
⅛ yard of accent fabric for Folded Flying Geese

Method
1. Cut strips of background for rows, starting at the top with the narrow rows. Take advantage of any striped fabric; cut alternate rows on the bias going in different directions. Also cut accent rectangles, which will form the Folded Flying Geese stitched into each row.

	Background	Contrasting Flying Geese Cuts
Row A	cut 4" × 1½" and 14" × 1½"	cut a 1½" × 2½" rectangle
Row B	cut 4" × 2" and 14" × 2"	cut a 2" × 3½" rectangle
Row C	cut 4" × 2½" and 14" × 2½"	cut a 2½" × 4½" rectangle
Row D	cut 4" × 3" and 14" × 3"	cut a 3" × 5½" rectangle
Row E	cut 4" × 3½" and 14" × 3½"	cut a 3½" × 6½" rectangle

2. Fold the rectangles in half, bringing the short sides together. Position the raw edges in the connecting seam of the companion cut strips. Place the fold ¼" down from the top (fig. 1.12). Pin all five rectangles in between the strips. Stitch each row together à la "kite" style, one right after the other in a sequence. Cut each strip apart; press the seam allowance open to relieve any bulk. On the front side, pull the corners into 45° angles toward the base, creating dimensional flying geese. The rectangular back of the collar will measure 10" × 17" plus seam allowances once these rows are stitched together.

3. To complete the collar tie ends, make a pattern from the schematic (fig. 1.13) that starts with a 1" header with a curve formed by a 4" radius to a 4½"-wide long extension that extends 22" downward. (Use the yardstick beam compass to create the curve.)

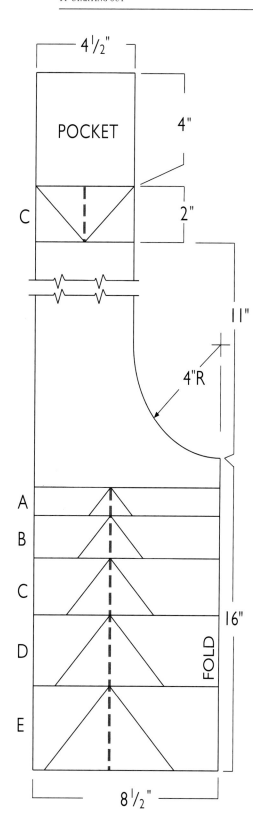

Figure 1.13

Cutting for pockets:

Cut 2 rectangles 6½" × 5" for facing.

Cut 2 rectangles 4½" × 5" for front panels.

Cut 4 squares 2½" (behind the Folded Flying Geese).

Cut 2 rectangles 2½" × 4½" (contrasting Folded Flying Geese).

Stitch together two sets of squares that include the Folded Flying Geese. Sew on the base, using 4½" × 5" rectangles below the Flying Geese rectangles. Face each section by sewing the 6½" × 5" rectangles to the top of each section. Place each at the end of the tie, aligning raw edges.

4. Cut a collar lining according to the pieced collar. Stitch a 2" folded bias around the entire collar. Hand stitch bias onto the backside of collar.

Optional Finish: Cut a lining according to sewn collar. Align right sides together. Stitch a ¼" seam on all sides, leaving about a 6" to 7" opening. Trim right-angle corners. Invert the collar through the opening. Sew opening closed.

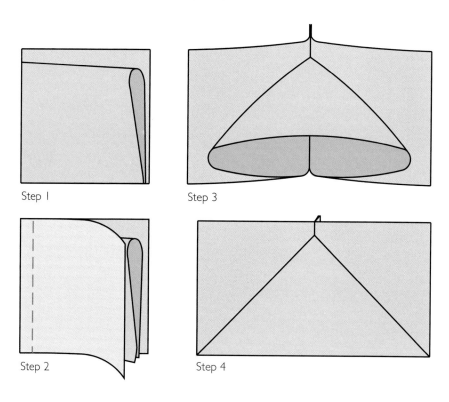

Step 1

Step 2

Step 3

Step 4

Figure 1.12

PROJECT: PASTEL PLACEMATS

Use the same cutting measurements as for the collar, but add an extra bottom row. Make double cuts for two mats. Cut lining and cotton batting for each: 14" × 17½". Finished size is 13½" × 17".

	Background	Contrasting Flying Geese Cuts
Row F	cut two 4" × 14" and two 4" × 4"	cut two 4" × 7½" rectangles

This time, stitch the folded rectangle into the right side of the background strips. The dimensional, open triangles become a pocket for silverware. Bind each placemat with matching bias cut 2½", or invert each placemat with a lining. Just think of the possibilities for this new, nifty technique.

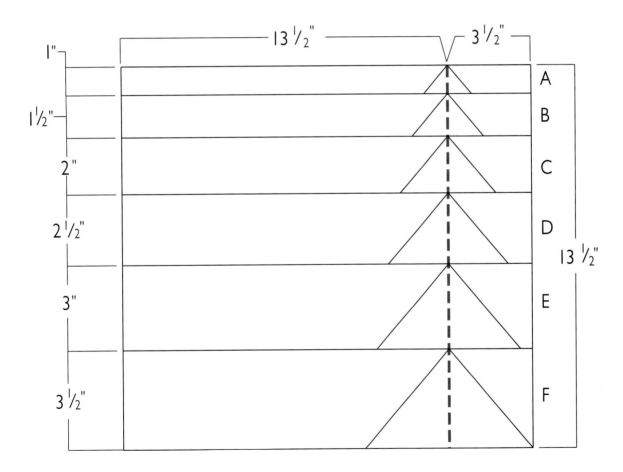

Figure 1.14

PROJECT: TRIANGLE TABARD

Utilizing Folded Flying Geese in a vest or tabard is another patchwork proposition. The vertical aspect is always appealing to the human form, as we are always anxious to elongate. I used denim and made the back the same as the front, with a bright lining. Size changes can be made according to longer or shorter strips, by adding more across the width, or by adjusting the side button closure. This tabard is a medium size.

Materials

⅔ yard of denim and lining
Thirty-four 2" × 3½" assorted calicoes for the rectangles
Bias cut accent fabric, 2¼" wide × 3½ yards long
2 buttons for the side closure

Method

1. Using the 1" grid diagram, make a sample tabard out of miserable material to accommodate your size figure. Alterations can be made here for a smaller size by shortening strips or reducing the number of strips across the tabard width. For larger sizes, add strips in length and width.

2. Follow the schematic to cut out 2"-wide strips of denim for the front and back. Cut duplicate strips to include both sides. The measurement given at the end of each strip indicates the length to cut. For the middle part, between the Folded Flying Geese, cut fourteen 8½" strips that are 2" wide.

3. Piece each row in duplicate as you insert the folded rectangle to form a Flying Geese triangle. Pin it open once sewn. Sew the rows together, keeping track of each row next to each other. Shape the front and back neck area according to the schematic and your figure. Stitch together the shoulders of the pieced tabard and the lining.

4. Place together the right sides of the lining and decorative top, and stitch around the neck area. Trim off excess seam allowance, clip the "V" front and back, and turn right side out. Finish off raw edges with the 2¼"-wide continuous bias.

5. For the button closure, fold four 5" denim squares into triangles. Satin stitch the raw edges and secure to the waist area of each side of the tabard. Place a buttonhole in each side with corresponding sewn button.

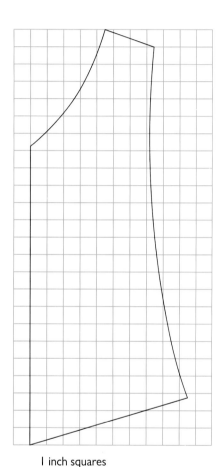

1 inch squares

Figure 1.15a

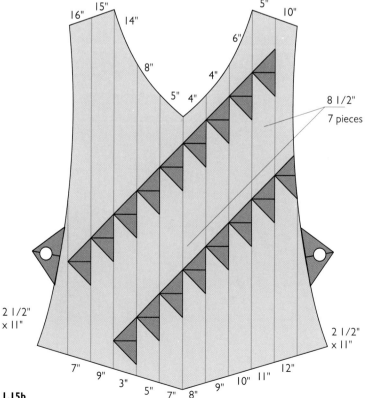

Figure 1.15b

2 Focus on Fabric

ODE TO FABRIC

Yes, we collect it,
we covet it,
we stroke it,
we hoard it,
we barter it,
we share it,
we stare at it,
we drive miles for it,
we color it,
we store it,
we wash and dry it,
and then we cut it apart only to sew it together again.
What would we do without it? Thank heavens for cotton!

FABRIC DICTIONARY

Are you a fabric-holic? How much do you spend on fabric in one year? That's our quilter's secret! From A to Z there is a wealth of fabric design. Examine all the varieties, then enhance your collection with some of these additional fabrics. So often students come to a workshop with fabric selections matching what they are wearing. So concentrate on buying a wide range of colors and designs from A to Z. Your quilts will take on a new life.

A is for Amish, African, Animal, and Architecture
B is for Batik, Background, and Border Prints
C is for Calicoes, Cruise, and Cheater Cloth
D is for Decorator Prints
E is for Elaborate
F is for Focus, Fun, Folk, and Floral
G is for Geometrics—Stripes, Pin Dot, Checks (printed and woven), Plaids (printed and woven), and Gingham Checks
H is for Hand-Dyed and Holiday
I is for Indian
J is for Juvenile and Jungle
K is for Kids
L is for Landscape (mountains, trees, and leaves)
M is for Muslin and Music

Tips for Choosing Fabric

- "Glasses off" is a good way to select fabric. If your selection has little contrast and seems to run together, then fabric choices are too close in value.
- Geometrics (plaids, stripes, checks, etc.) settle prints and add character to the selection. Also choose a variety of sizes and texture so prints are not all the same size.
- Black intensifies all colors.
- The minimum to buy of a "must have, but not sure where to put it" fabric is one yard.
- Solid-colored fabric leads to a more contemporary, modern style quilt.
- Unroll the fabric bolt at the store and view it at a distance to determine any repeat pattern that would take away from an overall quilt backing.

- If you own a quilt shop, cut off and save the first yard of every new bolt of fabric. Date, price, and indicate source on the label on the fabric. It can fill someone's emergency request later and will also help you when you want to order more.
- Cotton is the quilters' choice, but there is a place for other fabrics. Consider blends for baby and children's quilts, silk for glitz and glamour in wall hangings, and denim and corduroy for the rustic, folk look in a quilt.
- Wash fabric with a 3" square of white fabric to check for fading. Orvus® soap is made for washing fabric and the finished quilt, too. To set any dyes that continue to bleed, use ProRetayne®, a dye fixative. Vivid®, a nonchlorine bleach available

at your grocery store, works great for laundering any quilt that has a fading problem.
- Just partially dry fabric in the dryer. I let it air dry on a railing, coat hanger, or banister. While the piece is damp, stretch or "yank" it into shape by holding onto opposite corners. Engage a friend or puzzled husband for this task.
- Do not store your fabric in exposed light; even the fold can be affected. Keep it in an enclosed area where you can turn a light on and off for selection—and stroking.
- Remember, you can never have too much fabric!

N is for Nature (sky, water, and watercolor)

O is for One-Way versus Nondirectional Prints

P is for Paisley and Patriotic

Q is for Quilted-looking Fabric

R is for Recycled Fabrics

S is for Solids

T is for Texture and Toil

U is for Uglies

V is for VIP—our classics

W is for White on White

X is for EXTRA

Y is for Yardage

Z is for "Zingers"

PROJECT: PRINT COLOR WHEEL

I have a collection of books on color. I have taken color classes. I try to explain my color choices, but in the end I believe color decisions come from the heart. Evaluating quilts at shows, pictures of quilts in books and magazines, and even quilts made by your friends is the best way to determine your selection. Sometimes you just have to weed out what you don't want in order to determine what pleases you and what you want to live with in your home. Sometimes when you take that last stitch, stand back, and gaze at your quilt, you exclaim, "Why didn't I use a stronger shade of yellow?" Maybe that is why we keep making quilts—until we finally get it right!

A color wheel is a must to hang in your studio—especially if it's in prints.

Materials

½ yard of black fabric.

Two 4" white squares for the heart center

16" hoop

25" string to pull through back casing

Batting and backing cut to fit the pieced circular color wheel

4" square of print fabric for each of the 36 colors on the color wheel

Method

1. Cut twelve #1 template in black. Also cut a 3" × 53" band in black.

2. Cut twelve #3 template true color; cut twelve #4 template tints (lighter value of the true color); cut twelve #2 template shades (darker value of the true color).

3. Stitch each set of #1, #2, #3, and #4 fabrics together, keeping the wedges correct, with the proper colors next to one another. Stitch these into a circle, alternating seams on the backside as the wedges are sewn together.

4. With two layers of white fabric for the heart, trace the outline of the design. Machine embroider or hand embroider the words "Color Comes from the Heart." A permanent marking pen is an optional writing tool for the heart. Appliqué this onto the center of the color wheel. Trim any excess from the tint shades on the underside after the appliqué is complete. Layer color wheel, batting, and backing, and baste together in preparation for hand or machine quilting. After quilting, trim into an even circle.

5. Stitch the 3"-wide band around the outside and sew a ½" hem on the edge, with two openings 1" apart. Pull a string through the openings to gather the color wheel over a 16" hoop. Finish by securing the outside hoop. Hang in your sewing space as a constant reminder of the many quilt color options.

Groupie Guidelines

You can make this color wheel by yourself, but there is a benefit in making it in your quilt group. If there are twelve members, each member can pick one color, along with its tint and shade, and cut enough for every member. This way you do not have the responsibility of selecting all twelve colors along with their tints and shades. Of course, with only six members each person would choose two colors.

FIRST MEETING

Each quilter selects a color or colors for research and cutting. Cut the required templates from print cotton fabric (see step 2 under "Method"). Also, be prepared to give a report on your color. You might consider the following:

1. What temperature is your color?

2. Name three places where your color is seen most often.

3. What animal do you associate with your color?

4. Create a story, a fable, or a poem based on your color.

5. Show examples of successful and not so successful quilt results with your color.

This color wheel was a project at my Freedom Escape week in Weaverville, North Carolina, where I have taught the same students every winter for the past fourteen years. Naturally we have formed a strong bond as sisters in quilting. It's a great opportunity to concentrate on projects night and day for an extended time. As a serious, progressive teacher, I ran into a "snag" at the second meeting of this class. At the bewitching hour of the color reports, a fire drill interrupted our session! How clever, these quilters. They are always prepared to pull pranks on one another and the teacher.

SECOND MEETING

Naturally, come dressed in your chosen color. Give color reports and share color ideas. Exchange fabric so that each quilter receives a complete set of thirty-six colors. Cut out #1 template in black twelve times. Follow steps 3 through 5 under "Method" to finish the project.

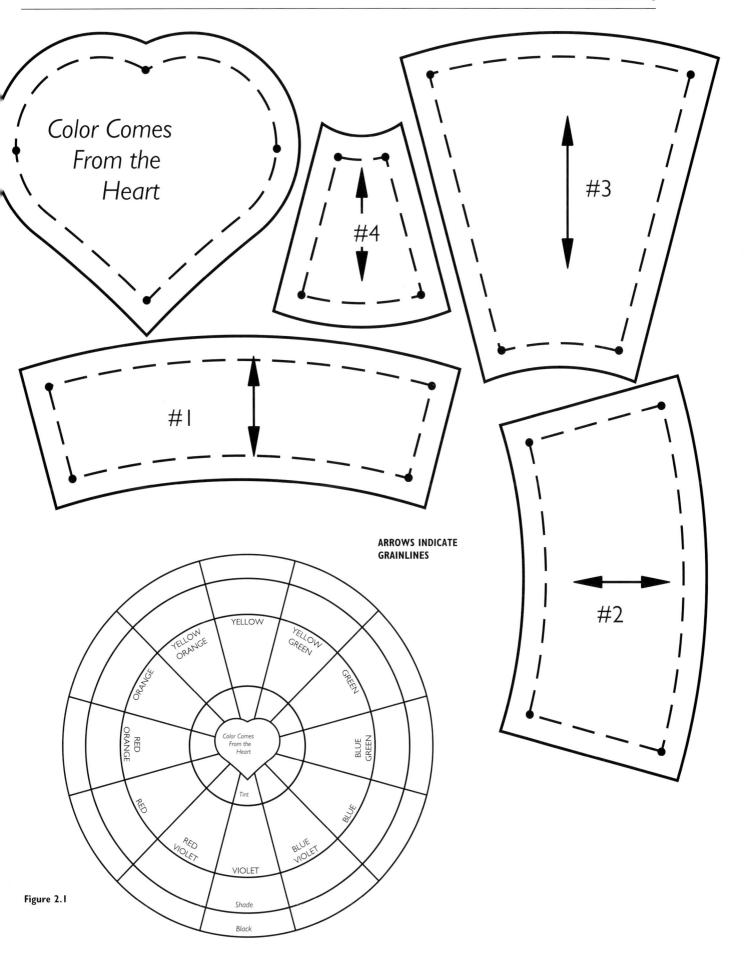

Color Comes
From the
Heart

#4

#3

#1

#2

ARROWS INDICATE
GRAINLINES

YELLOW

YELLOW
ORANGE

YELLOW
GREEN

ORANGE

GREEN

RED
ORANGE

BLUE
GREEN

Color Comes
From the
Heart

Tint

RED

BLUE

RED
VIOLET

BLUE
VIOLET

VIOLET

Shade

Black

Figure 2.1

PROJECT: PERCOLATOR PATCHWORK QUILT

Coffee pots on a quilt? Musical notes on a wall hanging? Sometimes the fabric itself becomes the stimulation for a quilt. Instead of starting with a design and searching for the fabric, just reverse the process. Let fabric be the inspiration!

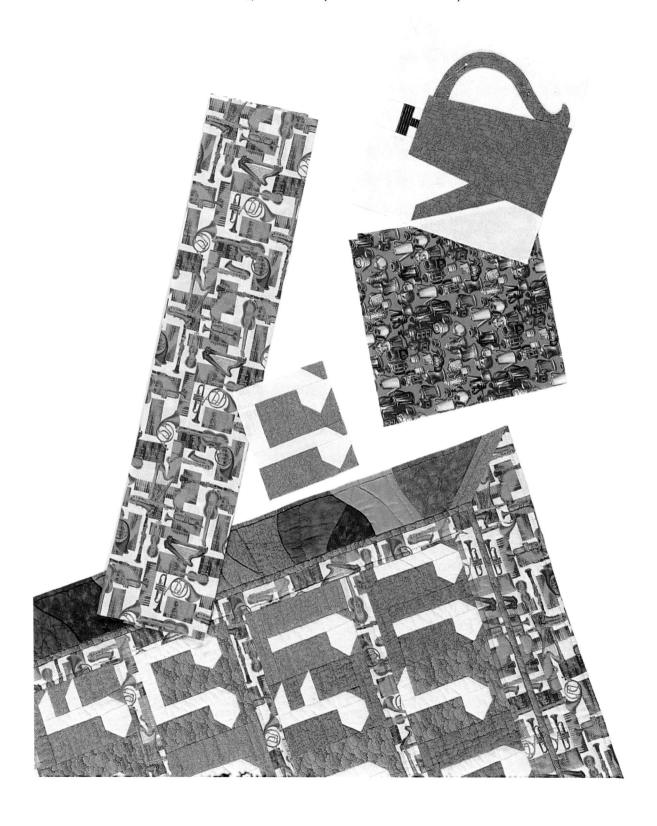

Fabric printed with coffee pots became the inspiration for a charity quilt, a joint effort by the Western North Carolina Quilters Guild and myself as a donation to the Education Foundation of Henderson County, North Carolina. What makes this quilt special are the unique handles on a variety of colorful coffee pots. Where else but in your hometown guild would you find twenty clever quilters to design this many different handles. Note that two members were left-handed, so the coffee pots are reversed. This is a lesson in designing your own block on gridded freezer paper, so follow step by step and learn all of the advantages. Finished quilt size is 77½" × 93".

Materials

3¼ yards of print fabric (See cutting schematic in fig. 2.2 for cutting directional fabric.)

Inside accent strips: cut two for top and bottom, 1½" × 59";
  cut two for the sides, 1½" × 76½".

Outside print borders: cut two for the top and bottom, 9" × 61½";
  cut two for the sides, 9" × 93½".

2¾ yards of white fabric for background

5⅓ yards for backing

Small napkins (check out your "next to new" shops):
  cut out twenty decorative corners.

Twenty random fabrics cut 13" square for coffee pots

¼ yard of black fabric for lid

32" square of fabric for the binding, cut into 2½" strips on bias or straight of grain

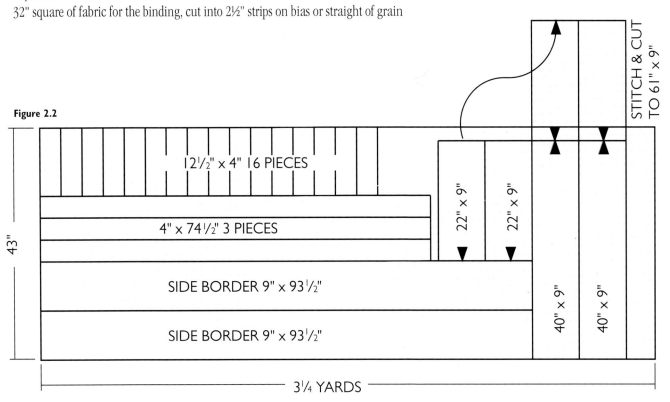

Figure 2.2

12½" × 4" 16 PIECES

4" × 74½" 3 PIECES

SIDE BORDER 9" × 93½"

SIDE BORDER 9" × 93½"

43"

22" × 9"

22" × 9"

40" × 9"

40" × 9"

STITCH & CUT TO 61" × 9"

3¼ YARDS

Grid Grip® Block Designing

For many years it has been my patchwork practice to make quilts based on the classic "hand-me-down" shapes. When repeating these geometric shapes, the calculator, rotary cutter, and speed sewing techniques have resulted in many quilts. However, sometimes I want to venture away from the everyday, reliable shapes. It has become easy to do since I discovered Grid Grip®, a tool that gave me a graph pad, template, and stitching line in one. I could explore new angles. As a teacher, I am pleased to pass on this idea. After all, patchwork is a puzzle of lines that come together with only a ¼" seam allowance in between.

The advantages of using Grid Grip®:

- The poly-coated, shiny, nongridded side adheres to fabric with a dry iron on cotton setting.
- The templates can be reused many times; simply re-iron.
- It provides a continuous graph pad for drafting.
- Coding each template once it is drawn gives the sequence of piecework. Mark any "crossover clues." These would be filled quarter-inch grids or notches that cross over a drawn line wherever color and templates change.
- The pattern edge creates a stitching line to follow once the 4" seam allowance has been added.
- The appliqué advantages are in Chapter 4.

- The grid of each template is synonymous with the fabric grainline, eliminating bias edges of blocks and designs.
- It's a great introductory tool for teaching patchwork to children.
- For hand piecing, the paper edge is firm enough to trace around as a sewing guide.
- Any cutting error should be patched with masking tape, not cellophane or plastic tape, as it can take repeated ironing.
- A good way to store used templates is to re-iron them onto fabrics.
- Grid Grip® may be enlarged by pressing overlapped edges together.

Method

Follow the drafting of the Percolator pattern step by step to understand the potential of Grid Grip®. The top lid B panel is quick-cut and pieced.

With a pencil and a 12" square of Grid Grip®, draw the percolator following the assigned grid. Remember the Grid Grip® becomes your drafting graph paper, template for cutting out fabric, and the stitching guide for perfect patchwork—and it can be reused many times. Since templates are pressed onto the backside of the fabric, the pattern is given reversed—the spout will point to the opposite side. Reverse the drawing, depending on which way you want the spout to point.

1. Cut a 12" square of Grid Grip®, or draw a 12" square on a full size of graph paper. Trace the 2½" top panel, B, which is quick pieced. The bottom portion of this block is the A panel (fig. 2.3a).

Figure 2.3a

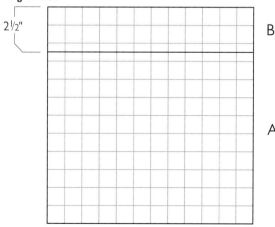

2½"

B

A

Step I

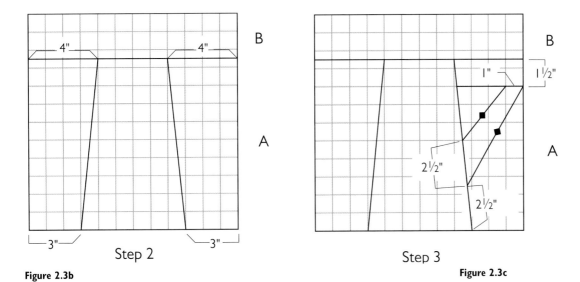

Step 2

Figure 2.3b

Step 3

Figure 2.3c

2. Trace the slanted lines of the coffee pot according to the dimensions (fig. 2.3b).

3. Draw the spout, following the measurements from the base of the block and the top section. Code each template and fill in any crossover clues (fig. 2.3c).

4. The top panel that includes the lid can be quick pieced, rather than using templates. The following cuts include enough pieces for all twenty blocks (fig. 2.4):

Cut forty light side rectangles—5½" × 3" (background fabric).

Cut two light strips 1¾" wide × 26" long and two dark strips (lid) 1¼" wide × 26" long. Sew the dark and light strips together twice and cut apart every 2½" to yield twenty partial tops 2½" square. Stitch the bottom pieces to this, once pieced (fig. 2.5a).

Cut two light strips 1¼" wide × 21" long and cut 1 dark strip (lid) 1" wide × 21" long. Sew a light strip on either side of the dark strip; press seam allowances toward the dark fabric; cut twenty rectangles 1" × 2½" (fig. 2.5b).

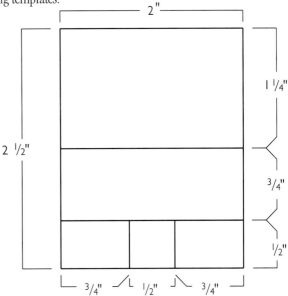

Figure 2.4

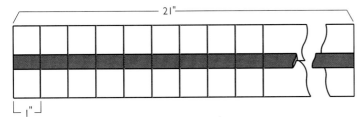

Figure 2.5a

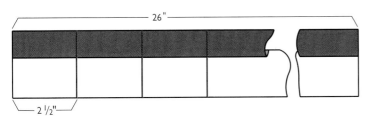

Figure 2.5b

Finishing Steps

1. Cut out the entire A panel of Grid Grip® once all the coding is in place. Press each template onto the backside of the respective fabric. Note that the grid aligns with the grainline of the fabric, so there will not be any bias edges. If using graph paper, trace each template onto plastic template material. Add a ¼" seam allowance on all sides before cutting out the patterns from plastic.

2. Stitch the A panel together twenty times. Follow the sequence of piecing (A1, then A2, etc.) as shown in fig. 2.6. Use the Grid Grip® as a sewing guide. Pin the seam allowances together and check to see that the grid from each template is even, then sew, being certain not to stitch through the paper on the underside. The paper may be re-pressed many times. Vary the colors of the percolator, or engage nineteen friends to select and stitch a block.

3. Stitch the top B panel twenty times and sew to the A panel. Cut out the handle design (use the suggested template in fig. 2.8 if you don't want to create your own) and apply it to the side opposite the spout. Appliqué this in place by unstitching any side portion where the handle should be secured. With blocks complete, "prune" or square up all the edges to an exact 12½" square. Position the blocks in a pleasing manner, balancing the color.

4. Place the long side of each napkin triangle on the center base of each coffee pot; baste in position. Pin the square end up against the block so it will not get caught in sashing connection. Stitch a 12½" × 4" sashing to sixteen of the coffee pots. As you add the print sashing, watch that any directional fabric is stitched correctly. Connect the vertical rows by sewing the remaining four coffee pots on the bottom rows. Stitch the long panels cut 4" × 74½" in between the four coffee pot rows.

5. Add the accent narrow strips on the top and bottom, then the sides. Complete the quilt top with the addition of print bottom and top borders, cut 9" × 61", and the side borders, cut 9" × 93½".

6. With a backing and batting cut, baste the three layers together. This quilt was machine quilted in the sashings and border areas with a meandering style. The block areas were hand quilted using various widths of masking tape to echo the percolator shape. Bind with a continuous bias or straight of the grain fabric cut 2½" wide, folded and stitched on the frontside and hand secured on the backside.

Hint

With any long rows of sashing, strips, or border, always fold and pinch to find the midpoint of the quilt and the panel to be added to distribute fabric evenly.

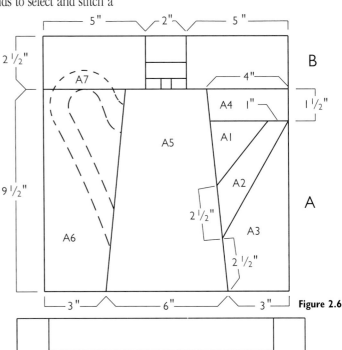

Figure 2.6

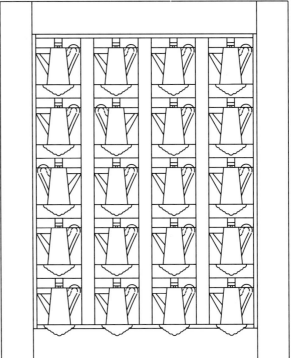

Figure 2.7

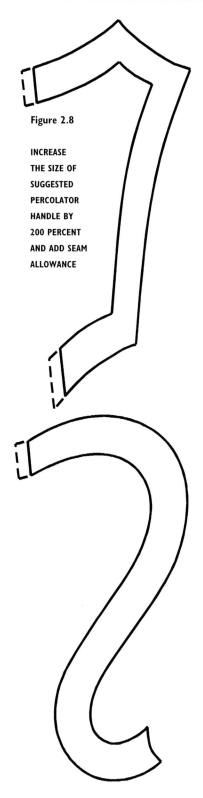

Figure 2.8

INCREASE
THE SIZE OF
SUGGESTED
PERCOLATOR
HANDLE BY
200 PERCENT
AND ADD SEAM
ALLOWANCE

PROJECT: PERCOLATOR PATCHWORK WALL HANGING

Finished size is 20" × 48". For a bright kitchen accent, make three coffee pot blocks for a horizontal wall hanging.

Materials

Three 12½" coffee pot blocks
Four print borders, cut 3½" × 12½"
Two top and bottom borders, cut 4½" × 48½"
Batting and backing, cut 21" × 49"
Binding made with a 20" square of fabric

Method

1. Complete the three coffee pot blocks. Attach diagonal cut napkin ends to each base.

2. Sew side borders between each block. Sew top and bottom wider borders.

3. Baste the batting and backing together, and hand quilt inside the coffee pot. (I used my walking [even-feed] foot to outline the coffee pot shape with machine stitching. To quilt the borders, I programmed "Java" and "Cup of Joe" on my sewing machine for accent quilt connections.) Bind the wall hanging using continuous bias cut 2½" wide.

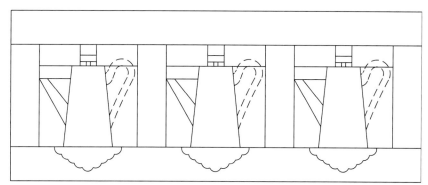

Figure 2.9

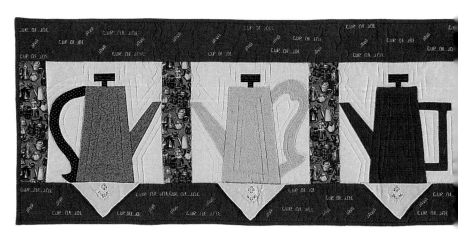

3 Design Details

Examine the quilts you want to make and look at the quilts you have already made. Can you identify the quilt category? Becoming more knowledgeable about quiltmaking means learning the basic categories, how the sections are divided, and what shapes determine the outcome. Of course, this could be a lifetime study, because there are thousands of quilt patterns, but understanding the basics has many advantages. Learning to distinguish blocks and overall quilt settings is a step toward quilt confidence. It aids in drafting, designing the next guild quilt, holding up your end of a conversation on quilting, and researching antique tops. Knowing the basic quilt categories will open many new doors.

DESIGN CATEGORIES

The following are the most basic quilt categories:

Medallion. Bands of pieced or unpieced rows radiate outward from a central design to form a quilt top.

Figure 3.1

Bar. The top is made up of elongated, vertical strips that alternate between pieced and unpieced rows.

Figure 3.2

All-over Pattern. This honeycomb design of hexagons, for example, relies on one or more shapes repeated. Another example is the Wedding Ring pattern.

Figure 3.3

Basic Four Patch. Any block pattern that is divided horizontally and vertically into four equal, or nearly equal, parts.

Figure 3.4

Basic Nine Patch. Any block pattern that is divided by two horizontal and two vertical seams, which creates nine parts, either squares or rectangles.

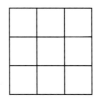

Figure 3.5

Twenty-five Patch Block. Any block pattern that is divided by four horizontal and four vertical seams to create twenty-five parts, either squares or rectangles.

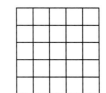

Figure 3.6

Diagonal Four Patch. Any block that is divided into four triangles by two intersecting diagonal lines.

Figure 3.7

Square within a Square. Any block that has an offset or on-point square within the boundaries of a larger square.

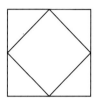

Figure 3.8

Log Cabin Block. A classic pattern based on rectangles added around a center square.

Figure 3.9

Fan Block. Any block based on a quarter-circle in one corner. This corner circle can be further divided into wedges.

Figure 3.10

Picture Blocks. Any patterns of realistic, recognizable designs such as baskets, houses, or trees.

Figure 3.11

Star Blocks. Diamond and triangle shapes radiating within the boundaries of a square or rectangle. These blocks can form 4-, 5-, 6-, 7-, or 8-pointed stars.

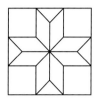 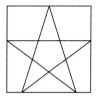

Figure 3.12a   **Figure 3.12b**

TECHNIQUE: SWIFT CUTTING OF ATTIC WINDOWS

An all-time favorite four patch block, Attic Windows (fig. 3.13), can now be readily cut and sewn using the ⅞" (.875") seam allowance addition for the diagonal end. Follow the measurements and diagrams for your size choice. The ⅞" addition allows you to cut a 45° angle off one end of the rectangle that includes the ¼" seam allowance on all sides (fig. 3.14). Adapt this block to any of the repeat quilt patterns for an entire quilt or a wall hanging. I use my feedsack material for this design. By trading through the mail, I have exchanged many 6" squares. (See Resources for the Feedsack Club address.) I determine the size of my block by utilizing as much of the 6" square as possible. The quarter sections will be 5", so my block will be 10" square. Experiment with the Attic Window block settings as in the following options (see figs. 3.15a–e).

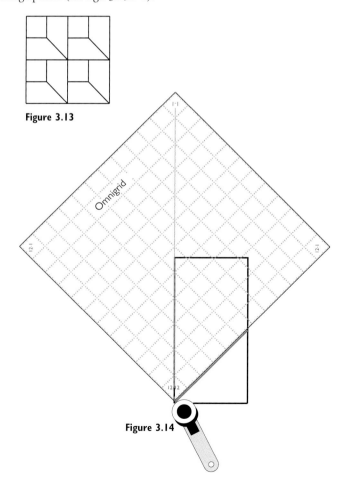

Figure 3.13

Figure 3.14

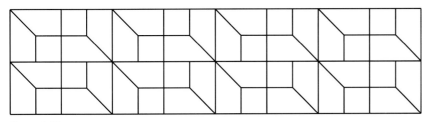

Figure 3.15a

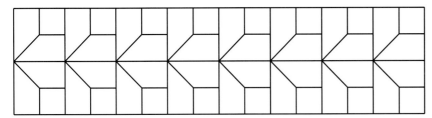

Figure 3.15b

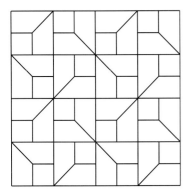

Figure 3.15c

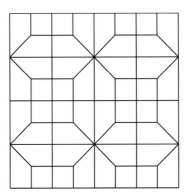

Figure 3.15d

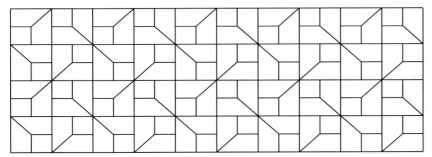

Figure 3.15e

4" Attic Window Block

Cut four 1½" corner squares. Cut four sets of different fabric (align right or wrong sides of fabric together) into rectangles 1½" × 2⅞". At one end of each rectangular set, cut a 45° angle.

6" Attic Window Block

Cut four 2" corner squares. Cut four sets of different fabric (align right or wrong sides of fabric together) into rectangles 2" × 3⅞". At one end of each rectangular set, cut a 45° angle.

8" Attic Window Block

Cut four 2½" corner squares. Cut four sets of different fabric (align right or wrong sides of fabric together) into rectangles 2½" × 4⅞" At one end of each rectangular set, cut a 45° angle.

10" Attic Window Block

Cut four 3" corner squares. Cut four sets of different fabric (align right or wrong sides of fabric together) into rectangles 3" × 5⅞". At one end of each rectangular set, cut a 45° angle.

PROJECT:
ANTIQUE MEDALLION QUILT — AN EIGHT-WEEK CLASS

The essence of traditional patchwork is featured in this medallion quilt. This is a sampler, of sorts, with a wealth of geometric shapes. I acquired this quilt top in a collection of quilts from the Charleston, South Carolina, area. I replaced a few patches and elongated

the top with additional pieced bands and an outer border to give this quilt a new life. The period fabrics add such character to each succeeding band as the quilt extends outward. Remaking classic quilts can present many challenges, but considering our new methods and updated tools, it becomes "a piece of cake." Consider, for this quilt, just how far you want to go. The center could be just a pillow top square, a beginner project. As the quilt expands outward, the quilt size as well as the degree of difficulty increases, from intermediate to advanced as the bands expand. Make this quilt as a round robin project with your "groupie" friends, or treat it as an eight-week quilting class. The fabric amounts are given separately for each of the eight bands. Finished size is 85½" × 76".

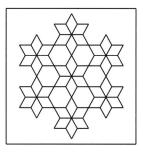

Figure 3.16a

cut 11³⁄₄" square

First Week

Make the center block (A), which includes seven 60° diamond stars connected by six hexagons (fig. 3.16a). Finished block size is 11¼".

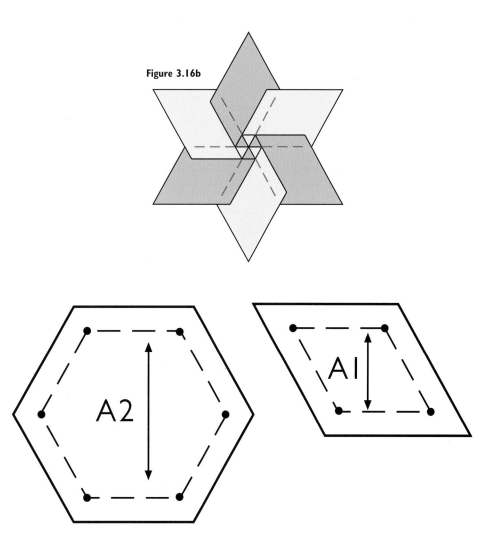

Figure 3.16b

Materials
⅓ yard of muslin, background fabric
⅛ yard of calico
⅛ yard of other calico

Cutting
Cut six 1" muslin hexagons (see template 2).
Cut twenty-one calico diamonds (see template 1).
Cut twenty-one other calico diamonds (see template 1).
Cut one 11¾" square muslin foundation.

Method
1. Machine or hand piece seven stars together. Alternate colors of each star point. Stitch just to the ¼" on the outside angles. Stitch each star in halves of three points each in order to have one long connecting seam between all six points. Keep all seam allowances on the backside going in the same direction. Release the initial center seam allowance to create a twirl for a softer intersection (see fig. 3.16b).
2. Position stars and hexagons in the proper setting and stitch star sides to each side of the hexagons.
3. Hand appliqué this unit onto the foundation.

Second Week

Make the Star Blocks (B), sixteen altogether, that frame the center square. Finished block size is 3¾".

Materials
½ yard of muslin, background fabric
¼ yard of calico
¼ yard of other calico

Cutting
Cut eight calico and eight other calico 2⅜" squares for centers.

Cut eight calico and eight other calico 3¾" squares, then cut these apart on the right angles and the diagonal angles. This yields small calico triangles to be sewn onto the muslin triangles to form the Flying Geese segment for each star side (fig. 3.17b).

Cut sixteen 3⅛" muslin squares, then cut these apart on the diagonal. Stitch the small calico triangles onto each side of the diagonal to form Flying Geese (fig. 3.17c).

Figure 3.17a

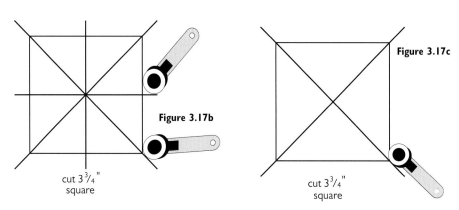

cut 3³⁄₄"
square

Figure 3.17b

Figure 3.17c

cut 3³⁄₄"
square

Cut sixteen 2⅜" muslin squares. Press this square in half for each quarter section, then cut apart on the quarter sections. This yields sixty-four squares.

Method

1. Stitch thirty-two Flying Geese rectangles for each calico star—four sets for each Star Block. Align the 45° point first to stitch. Press seams to the muslin. Add other calico triangle, press seams outward, and trim off dog ears (fig. 3.17d, step 1).

2. Sew a Flying Geese rectangle to each side of eight calico and each side of eight other calico squares (fig. 3.17d, step 2).

3. Sew squares on either side of the remaining Flying Geese rectangles, and then sew these to either side of the center star rectangle (fig. 3.17d, steps 3 and 4).

4. Sew these blocks into two rows of three blocks to stitch on either side of center medallion. Sew the remaining blocks into two rows of five blocks each and stitch to the other two sides (fig. 3.17e).

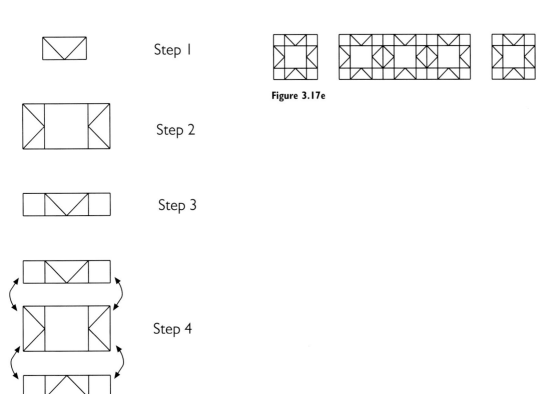

Step 1

Step 2

Step 3

Step 4

Figure 3.17e

Figure 3.17d

Third Week
Make the quarter-square triangles (C), twenty-eight altogether, that frame the Star Blocks from row B. Finished block size is 1⅝". These are separated by bars.

Figure 3.18a

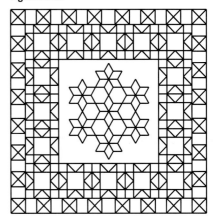

Materials
⅛ yard of muslin, background fabric
⅛ yard each of calico, other calico, and dark calico

Cutting
Cut calico aligned with muslin into seven 2⅞" squares.
Cut other calico aligned with muslin into seven 2⅞" squares.
Cut twenty-four bars from dark fabric, 2⅛" × 1¾". Cut four center bars, 2⅛" × 2".

Method
1. Draw a diagonal line on the backside of all sets of muslin/calico and muslin/other calico. Stitch a ¼" seam on each side of the line, cut apart, trim dog ears, and press seams toward the calico (fig. 3.18b). Realign these squares made of two half-square triangles with right sides together, seams staggered, and draw another diagonal line. Stitch on either side of these diagonals; cut apart and trim dog ears to yield fourteen quarter-square triangles of calico and fourteen of other calico (fig. 3.18c).

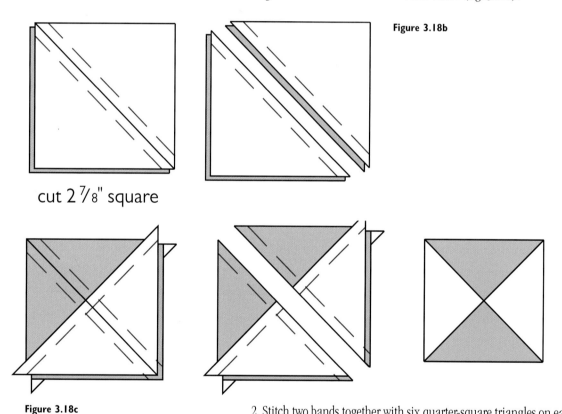

Figure 3.18b

cut 2 ⅞" square

Figure 3.18c

2. Stitch two bands together with six quarter-square triangles on each side separated by bars. Place the 2"-wide bar in the center. Sew these to either side of row B.

3. Stitch the remaining quarter-square triangles together with bars in between, placing the 2"-wide bar in each center (fig. 3.18d). Sew these on the other two sides of B.

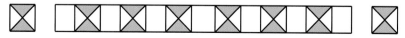

Figure 3.18d

Fourth Week

Make a band of split Flying Geese segments (D), fifty-six altogether, with corner Star Blocks. Finished size is 1½" × 3", with 3" corner Star Blocks.

Figure 3.19a

Materials

½ yard of muslin, background fabric
⅛ yard each of calico and other calico

Cutting

Corner Blocks

Cut four 2" calico squares.

Cut four 3¼" calico squares. Then cut these apart on the quarter sections and the diagonal. This yields thirty-two triangles.

Cut four 2¾" muslin squares into quarters—sixteen squares.

Split Flying Geese Cuts

Cut four 3⅞" calico squares aligned with muslin.

Cut four 3⅞" other calico squares aligned with muslin.

Cut seven squares of calico and other calico, 4¾". Then cut these apart on the diagonal to yield fifty-six calico and fifty-six other calico.

Cut fourteen 4¾" muslin squares. Cut apart on the quarter sections and then the diagonal to yield 112 triangles.

Cut eight calico bands 1" × 3½".

Method

1. Corner stars: refer to method instructions for row B, making four corner stars.

2. Draw diagonal and quarter section lines on the backside of all muslin/calico and muslin/other calico squares. Stitch on either side of all diagonal lines only, but then cut apart on all lines to yield thirty-two half-square triangles of each calico (fig. 3.19b). (Throw away four squares of each color, or save for another project.) Save twenty-eight for each color.

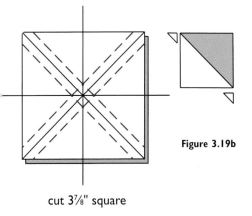

Figure 3.19b

cut 3⅞" square

3. Sew calico and other calico triangles to each side of the half-square triangles to yield twenty-eight split Flying Geese triangles for each calico color.

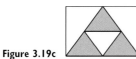

Figure 3.19c

4. Add the muslin triangles to each side to form fifty-six rectangles (fig. 3.19c).

5. Sew fourteen of these units together for each side. Add the narrow 1" bands of calico at each end to extend the length. Sew two bands on opposite sides of row C. Add Star Blocks to the end of the remaining rows and sew to the other C sides (fig. 3.19d).

Figure 3.19d

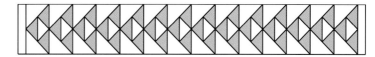

Fifth Week

Make a triangle zigzag border (E) using updated Seminole techniques. Finished size is 3" × 28"; Star Blocks are 3" corner squares.

Figure 3.20a

Materials
½ yard of muslin, background fabric
½ yard of calico

Cutting
Corner Blocks
Cut four 2" calico squares.

Cut four 3¼" calico squares. Then cut these apart on the quarter sections and the diagonal. This yields thirty-two triangles.

Cut four 2¾" muslin squares and cut apart on the diagonal to yield sixteen triangles.

Cut four 2½" muslin squares and cut into quarters for sixteen squares.
Zigzag Border

Cut muslin and calico strips on the bias, 58" × 2⅝" four times. Piece these strips on the diagonal. Work in four separate sections for each side.

Method

1. Stitch Star Block corners the same as row B.

2. Stitch the four sets of calico and muslin together. Use spray sizing on these bias strips to add stability for stitching. Press seams toward the dark calico. Cut strips apart every 2⅝" to yield twenty-two sections for each band (fig. 3.20b).

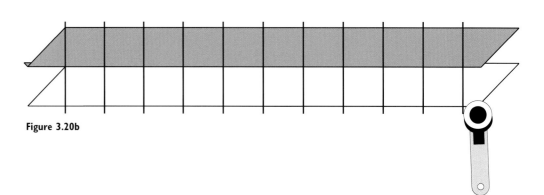

Figure 3.20b

3. Stitch two rows of eleven segments together, dropping the muslin down so the raw edge is ¼" from the center seam. Do this three more times. Cut off the triangular excess on each side, leaving a quarter-inch seam allowance (fig. 3.20c).

Figure 3.20c

4. Reposition the diagonal seam lines to up with the middle of the triangle. Stitch two bands together for a zigzag 3½" border. Repeat this three more times. Trim each band to 28½" to fit the previous border.

5. Stitch a border to opposite sides of row D. Add the Star Blocks onto the ends of the remaining two rows and sew to the other two sides of row D (fig. 3.20d).

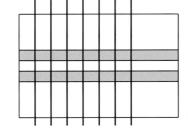

Figure 3.20d

Sixth Week

Make a nine patch offset block (F) row via the Seminole technique. Finished size is 34" × 4"; corner Star Blocks are 4".

Materials
1 yard of muslin, background fabric
¼ yard each of calico and other calico

Cutting
Corner Star Blocks
Cut four 2½" calico squares.
Cut four 3¾" calico squares. Then cut apart on the diagonal and quarter section to yield thirty-two triangles.
Cut four 3¼" muslin squares on the diagonal to yield sixteen triangles.
Cut four 3" muslin squares into quarter sections to yield sixteen squares.
Seminole Technique: Offset Nine Patch
For each side, cut and stitch the following I, II, and III bands. Repeat each of these three more times for each side.
Band I: Cut muslin on bias 3⅜" × 9⅝".
Cut medium calico 1⅜" × 9⅝".
Cut muslin 1⅜" × 9⅝".
Cut medium calico 1⅜" × 9⅝".
Cut muslin on bias 3⅜" × 9⅝".
(Fig. 3.21b)

Figure 3.21a

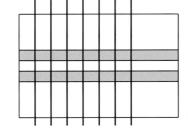

Figure 3.21b

Band II: Cut muslin on bias 3⅜" × 19¼".
    Cut medium calico 1⅜" × 19¼".
    Cut muslin 1⅜" × 19¼".
    Cut dark calico 1⅜" × 19¼".
    Cut muslin on bias 3⅜" × 19¼".
    (Fig. 3.21c)

Figure 3.21c

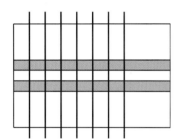

Figure 3.21d

Band III: Cut muslin on bias 3⅜" × 8¼".
    Cut dark calico 1⅜" × 8¼".
    Cut muslin 1⅜" × 8¼".
    Cut dark calico 1⅜" × 8¼".
    Cut muslin on bias 3⅜" × 8¼".
    (Fig. 3.21d)

Method

1. Stitch the Star Block corners following instructions for row B.

2. Stitch bands together in the order in which they are cut. Take a ¼" seam allowance. Press all seams in one direction.

3. Cut each band apart 1⅜". Band I yields seven strips, Band II yields fourteen strips, and Band III yields six strips.

4. Sew these bands together, alternating between Bands I, II, III, II, but this time turn the band upside down. I, II (turn again), III, etc. Complete the remaining three bands (fig. 3.21e).

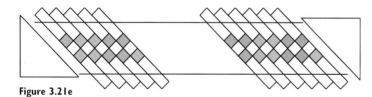

Figure 3.21e

5. Trim off equal amounts at each side to leave a band 4½" wide × 34½" long. Stitch a muslin triangle onto the opposite corners to square off the band. Sew two bands on the previous rows, E. Sew the Star Blocks on each end of the remaining offset nine patch rows, and sew these on opposite sides of E (fig. 3.21f).

Figure 3.21f

Seventh Week

Make a Flying Geese row (G) with 112 segments, 28 on each side. Finished size is 3" × 42". The corners use a 3" Star Block pattern.

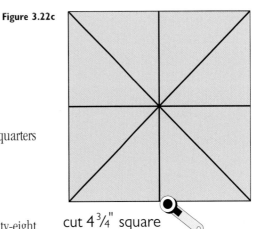

Figure 3.22a

Materials

½ yard of muslin

assorted calicoes left over from other rows — ½ yard total

Cutting

Follow the Star Block cutting and method of assembly for rows D and E.

For Flying Geese rectangles, cut seven assorted calicoes into 4¼" squares and divide these into twenty-eight triangles on the diagonal (fig. 3.22b).

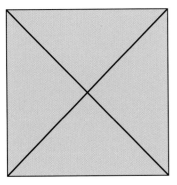

Figure 3.22b

cut 4 ¼" square

Figure 3.22c

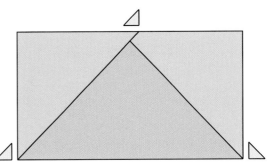

cut 4 ¾" square

Cut seven 4¾" muslin squares into triangles; cut these on the diagonal and quarters also (fig. 3.22c).

Method

1. Stitch a muslin triangle on either side of larger calico triangle to form twenty-eight rectangles. Press seams outward, away from the print triangle, and prune off any dog ears (fig. 3.22d). Do this step three more times for each side.

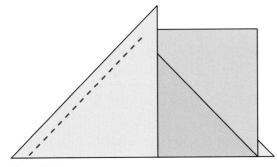

Figure 3.22d

2. With each of the twenty-eight segments stitched, sew two bands to opposite sides of the quilt, row F. Sew the Star Blocks onto each end of the remaining rows (fig. 3.22e). Sew these onto the remaining sides of row F.

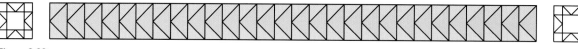

Figure 3.22e

Eighth Week

Make thirty-six LeMoyne Star Blocks (H), 6" square. This includes four Star Blocks for the corners also. Finished size is 48" × 6".

Figure 3.23a

Materials
½ yard of muslin, background fabric
1 yard of calico
1 yard of other calico

Cutting
Cut 144 2¼" muslin squares.

Cut thirty-six 3¾" muslin squares, divided on the diagonal to yield 144 triangles (fig. 3.23b).

Cut eight diamonds (four of calico and four of another calico) for each of the thirty-six Star Blocks, using the diamond template.

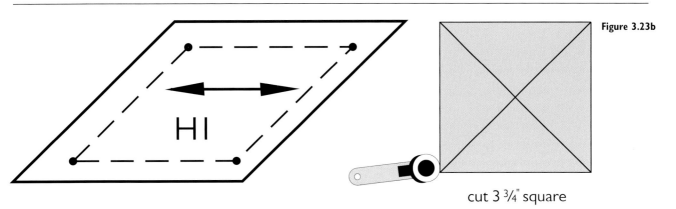

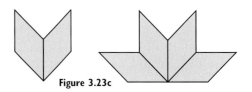

Figure 3.23b

cut 3 ¾" square

Method

1. Piece the Star Block by sewing two contrasting diamonds together four times. Stitch these into two halves (fig. 3.23c), and then, alternating closed seams, stitch across the two units. Stop, backstitch at the ¼" on all outside right angles of the star. Release the seam allowance in the center to twirl the intersection (figs. 3.23d–f).

Figure 3.23c

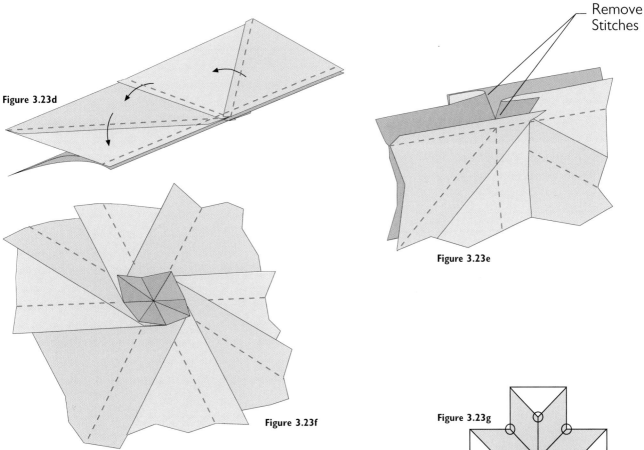

Figure 3.23d

Remove Stitches

Figure 3.23e

Figure 3.23f

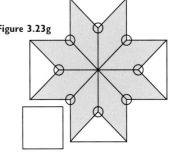

Figure 3.23g

2. Set in the triangles between the star points, aligning the 45° angles and backstitching at the inside right angle (fig. 3.23g).

3. Sew the corner squares, aligning the straight edge of the previous triangle as a guide (fig. 3.23h). Backstitch at the quarter-inch.

Figure 3.23h

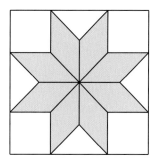

4. Sew units of eight Star Blocks together. Sew two of these on the previous row G (fig. 3.23i). Stitch Star Blocks onto the ends of the remaining bands, and sew these onto the other sides.

 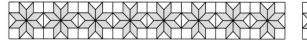

Figure 3.23i

Border Additions

On opposite ends of the quilt, pieced bands with 3" quarter-square triangles elongate the medallion panel. Between the squares are narrow bands of calico.

Figure 3.24

Materials

⅛ yard of muslin

¼ yard of light calico

⅛ yard of dark calico plus remnants from previous pieced bands

Cutting

Cut eighteen 3¾" muslin and eighteen 3¾" dark calico squares. Align these fabrics together before cutting out in preparation for quick sewing.

Cut eighteen scrap calico bands 1⅜" × 30". Cut these bands into 3" strips to be sewn in between the pieced units.

Cut two strips 2" × 60½" (piece sections with a diagonal seam).

Method

1. Draw a diagonal line on the backside of each muslin square that has been aligned with a dark calico. Stitch on either side of this line; cut apart; trim dog ears. Press seams toward the dark calico and realign with contrasting triangles. With another drawn diagonal line, stitch again on opposite sides of the triangle, cut apart, press, and trim off dog ears. Sew the 1⅜" strips in between the quarter-square triangles to a length of 60½".

2. Sew the 2"-long strips on either end of the quilt top. Add the pieced band after the strip addition.

Final Border Addition

First Border. Cut two strips 1¾" × 62½"—top and bottom.

Cut two strips 1¾" × 72"—sides.

Second Border. Cut two strips 3" × 67½"—top and bottom.

Cut two strips 3" × 77"—sides.

Third Border. Cut two strips 5" × 76½"—top and bottom.

Cut two strips 5" × 86"—sides.

Finishing. This antique quilt was quilted by Marie Detwiler. It has outline quilting lines that echo the pieced segments. Simple quilting lines are needed here, since there are a lot of seams and a complex design. A 31" square is required to make the continuous bias binding for this quilt.

4 Appliqué Options

For me, as a teacher, the opportunity to travel abroad only reinforces my love of quilt-making. With so many people stitching, how can we be wrong? What a joy to discover that other people have a heritage of needlework and that sewing is just as important in their lives. When I was in France, it was appropriate to teach appliqué, as the word itself originates from the French word that means "to apply or put something on top of something else."

THE APPLIQUÉ STITCH

Appliqué stitches are applied with the needle pointing to the left for right-handed persons (opposite for left-handed persons). The option for application is to appliqué looking over the figure or to appliqué looking into the figure to be attached to the foundation. See figs. 4.1. and 4.2 to understand the steps toward successful appliqué.

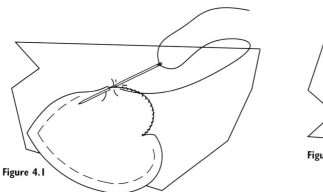

Figure 4.1

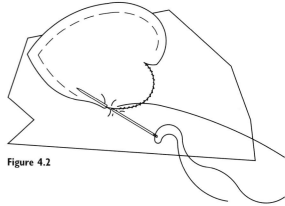

Figure 4.2

First, using a single strand of thread that matches the appliqué figure, start by pulling the knotted thread from the backside under the folded edge. Insert the needle into the very edge of the fold and pull through.

Second, insert the needle into the foundation exactly under where the thread has been inserted into the above fold. Take a small (⅛" x ¼") stitch, coming up into the edge of the fold again.

Appliqué depends on the amount of time you want to spend on your shape and the look you desire for the end result. Some hints and tips to consider:

- Combining various techniques on one project is readily accepted today. In fact, your quilt becomes more interesting, like having extra added attractions. Once a shape is appliquéd with hand stitching, an outline stem stitch in black can be added, or various shapes within one project can utilize more than one technique.

- Various weights of fabric respond to techniques differently, so try a sample first.
- Recognize that sometimes it takes more than one step to complete a cutout shape. For instance, a running stitch on the raw edge pulled around a cardboard circle can evenly pull excess seam allowance in place before applying it onto the foundation.
- Spray sizing applied on the seam allowance and then pressed into place over an ironable template (cardboard or plastic) sets the excess fabric in place firmly.
- Use a light box for tracing and template placement.
- For symmetrical designs on a square, fold and press foundation on the diagonal and the quarter. These crease lines aid in pinning shapes in place.
- Lightly trace the entire design on the foundation with a pencil. This might mean folding and refolding the foundation to retrace original setups that are mirror-image shapes. These lines help for needle turn applications.
- Consider how the raw edges will be turned under. Either baste them under before application, or pin shapes in place and needle turn as you attach each figure.
- When hand basting seam allowances in place, start with a knot of a single thread sewn on the front for easy removal.
- Trace around template on the fabric right side to reveal actual turn under line. A Grid Grip® template ironed in place here works well, since you can trace around the edge and then cut out the shape, allowing a narrow (between ⅛" and ¼") seam allowance.
- Narrow, continuous folded bias can be hand or machine stitched on top of the raw edge of any larger shape for an easy finish.
- An easy way to turn under the seam allowance of each shape is to stitch around the entire shape with used dryer sheets aligned with the right side of the fabric. Take a very small stitch in order to then slit the backside, which allows an inverting process to take place.
- Acute points for appliqué are best stitched by trimming the seam allowance to ⅛" for a narrower seam. Appliqué up to the point on one side and then needle turn the excess under with the needle point or a wet toothpick. Depending on the fabric weight, the point needs to be turned under first and then the adjacent side is appliquéd, or vice versa.
- Inside right angles need to be snipped up to the turn under seam. A wet toothpick and a small amount of glue stick help to keep wandering threads in place. A couple of extra stitches also help to anchor this turn.
- Bias strips are used in appliqué for stems and accent lines. Bias can be store-bought but is most often made to coordinate with the other fabrics. Bias bars are tools that come in various widths and are used as pressing bars. Simply cut the width required (doubled plus ¼") plus the length, and with the wrong sides together, sew a ⅛" seam allowance. Pull the bias bar through this tube and press, with the seam centered on the backside. Keep sliding the fabric bias through the bars for a continuous flat bias. For the ½" Romance of the Roses bias strips, cut the width 1¼".

Tips for the Traveling Quilter

- **Find a quilting pen pal. It's a great way to keep in touch with new techniques and to trade fabrics. Soon you will be traveling to visit.**
- **Watch for foreign travel through quilt magazines that includes tours, cruises, and conventions that inspire and instruct.**
- **Adopt a faraway sister guild for your hometown guild. What an opportunity to share stitching ideas between cultures.**
- **When traveling, take small notions and "goodies" to leave as favors.**
- **Check the phone directory at each new town for fabric and quilt shops.**
- **Invitations into quiltmakers' homes are the best opportunities to understand how they quilt and see their cloth results.**
- **Two cameras are a great indulgence—one for slides to share with the hometown guild and one for pictures.**

ROMANCE OF THE ROSES

The following patterns are classic, traditional appliqué blocks based on 12" squares; they offer a sampler effect for wall hangings or full-size quilts. I have used each of these blocks to illustrate a different technique. Partial appliqué stitching was made by Alice Wortman. Try all nine methods given here, or use your favorite method for each pattern. Follow the square schematics along with the cloth samples in progress, as a guide. Templates for the roses appear after the description of the nine techniques (fig. 4.12). The coding for each appliqué template is numbered according to the first shape to be applied, on up to the last shape to be applied. Note that in each case the foundation crease becomes a starting point.

Freezer paper has become a popular tool for appliqué application. The gridded form is especially useful when the shape is large, so the fabric grainline can be aligned with the foundation. With the background fabric cut away, quilting becomes easier through three layers instead of the extra layer of fabric. The first four blocks present freezer paper methods.

Bonded, press-on interfacing is another appliqué option. It's fast, easy, and appropriate for garments and quick wall hangings, but quilting is inhibited because a stiffer surface is created where the appliqué figure is applied.

Materials

¼ yard selection of five to six fabrics (include green)

Cut nine 12¾" foundation squares (trimmed to 12½" after appliqué is applied). Fold and crease each square on the diagonal and the quarter section for ease in appliqué placement. Press with a dry iron on cotton setting.

Select your favorite quilt or wall hanging setting and consult fabric amounts.

Lancaster Rose

Seam allowances pressed onto the shiny side of Grid Grip®.

1. Cut out the appliqué shape, allowing a full ¼" seam allowance. With the Grid Grip® appliqué template (without seam allowance) placed on the back of the fabric and the shiny, poly-coated side up, press the seam allowance onto the Grid Grip®. A pointed iron on medium, cotton setting aids in positioning the fabric over the paper. For any concave curves, snip the fabric to release the area. For any convex curves, cut out a V shape in several areas.

2. With the Grid Grip® in place, appliqué each shape in place on the foundation, positioning the shapes on the quarter section crease lines. Remove the paper inside by slitting the back behind each figure and pulling out the template.

Lancaster Rose
L1   (4)
L2   (4)
L3   (4)
L4   (1)
L5   (1)

Figure 4.3

Hollyhock Wreath

Grid Grip® pressed onto the template frontside.

1. Press Grid Grip® onto the frontside of cutout fabric appliqué shapes. Pin or tack each appliqué shape in place on the diagonal lines of the foundation to allow a needle turn application. Keep an iron nearby, as the warmth of your hand will release the template as you appliqué.

2. Carefully turn under the seam allowance with the needle point as you adhere each figure to the foundation. Tip: Keep a pin centered through all layers to eliminate any "pouching up" of the appliqué shape.

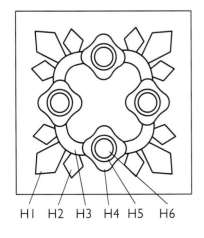

Hollyhock Wreath

H1	(4)
H2	(8)
H3	(4)
H4	(4)
H5	(4)
H6	(4)

H1 H2 H3 H4 H5 H6

Figure 4.4

President's Wreath

Grid Grip® pressed onto the backside.

1. Press the Grid Grip® onto the backside of each shape and cut out, allowing a seam allowance on all sides. Draw a centered 8½" circle on the foundation. Position the appliqué shapes on the pressed diagonal lines and the circle guides of the foundation.

2. Needle turn plus ironing seam allowances over the edge does help in this process. You can even make a firmer, stronger template by ironing two freezer papers together. Also, hand basting through the paper template is an option. Once the seam allowance has been pressed into place, the paper can be removed. If it is left on, it will have to be removed by slitting the foundation backside after the complete appliqué attachment is done.

Figure 4.5

P3 P6 P5 P4 P2 P1

President's Wreath
P1 (8)
P2 (24)
P3 (8)
P4 (4 - 1/2" x 5 1/4" Bias Strip)
P5 (4)
P6 (4)

Rose of Sharon

One of my favorite appliqué methods results in an overall single surface. This is especially good for large shapes where more quilting is placed inside.

    1. Press the cutout paper template onto the right side of the cloth shape, allowing a ¼" seam allowance around each shape. Situate the cutout fabric shape onto the diagonal crease lines of the foundation and machine stitch, twelve stitches per inch with coordinated thread, next to the paper template.

    2. With the lip appliqué scissors, cut away the excess up to the Grid Grip® template. Remove the paper template.

    3. Place a paper or appliqué stabilizer underneath the foundation and zigzag the appliqué shapes in place with a matching thread covering the original straight stitch. Cut away the foundation up to the zigzag stitch underneath each shape for a continuous single surface.

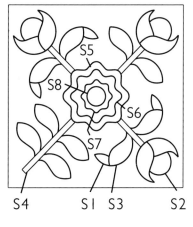

Rose of Sharon
S1 (4)
S2 (3)
S3 (16)
S4 (4 - 1/2" x 4 1/2" Bias Strip)
S5 (1)
S6 (1)
S7 (1)
S8 (1) **Figure 4.6**

Whig Rose

Machine buttonhole stitch.

1. Press the fabric to be cut out with spray sizing to add body and firmness. Press a Grid Grip® template onto the fabric backside; cut out the appliqué shape exactly up to the raw edge, rather than adding a seam allowance. Remove the Grid Grip®.

2. Position shapes following the diagonal crease lines, and with a narrow buttonhole stitch, secure each shape to the foundation. Matching thread works best, but an accent color can be introduced. Some buttonhole stitches can be reversed, creating a mirror image. A narrow, but wide zigzag, stitch is an optional stitch.

Figure 4.7

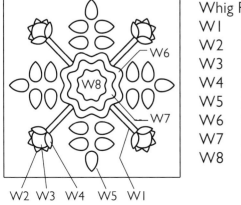

Whig Rose
W1   (4 - 1/2" x 3 3/4" Bias Strip)
W2   (16)
W3   (4)
W4   (8)
W5   (20)
W6   (1)
W7   (1)
W8   (1)

North Carolina Rose

Edge running stitch.

   1. Draw a centered 7½" circle on the foundation. With the raw edges of all shapes basted under in place, appliqué each one onto the foundation. Note the main flowers will align with the quarter section crease lines. Use a matching thread and make your running stitch very small so it can run right on the very edge as it goes through to the foundation. Dryer sheet used as a lining for shapes.

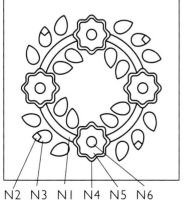

N2 N3 N1 N4 N5 N6

North Carolina Rose
N1   (4 - 1/2" x 4 1/4" Bias Strip)
N2   (4)
N3   (20)
N4   (4)
N5   (4)
N6   (4)

Figure 4.8

Radical Rose

Broderie Perse on raw edge.

1. A popular method of appliqué uses either black buttonhole thread or a matching, single-strand thread. Cut out the appliqué shape up to the template edge without any excess seam allowance. Spray sizing gives fabric more stability and body.

2. Position all shapes on the diagonal crease lines and reverse the hand buttonhole stitch to reveal a narrow edge with the long thread in the outside ditch.

Figure 4.9

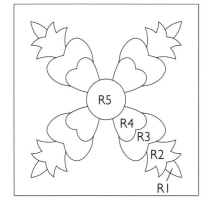

Radical Rose
R1   (4)
R2   (4)
R3   (4)
R4   (4)
R5   (1)

Great Grandmother's Rose

Machine blind hem stitch with monofilament thread.

1. With turned-under seam allowances, position each shape in place onto the foundation, aligning both the diagonal and quarter section crease lines.

2. Place monofilament, clear thread on the top and matching bobbin thread below in sewing machine. Use a blind hem stitch next to the edge. Adjust machine stitch to have a straight stitch in the ditch that alternates with a tiny zigzag. Keep shape in place with a center pin or it will not stay flat.

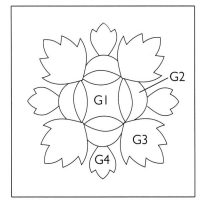

Great Grandmother's Rose

G1 (4)
G2 (4)
G3 (4)
G4 (4)

Figure 4.10

Ohio Rose

Reverse appliqué.

1. Trace the complete pattern of the shapes, setting the design by the quarter section press lines, onto the foundation. Pin or baste the new fabric to be added under the foundation, right side up.

2. Adding a seam allowance to turn under, clip out the shape on the foundation, leaving a small seam allowance. Either hand or needle turn any seam allowance underneath, revealing all of the fabric and the appliqué shape.

3. For machine application, stitch a single straight line first as a stabilizer, then cut out appliqué shape. Place a stabilizer underneath and use a very narrow satin stitch to complete the raw edges. It is possible to straight stitch through a paper pattern and then remove the paper.

Figure 4.11

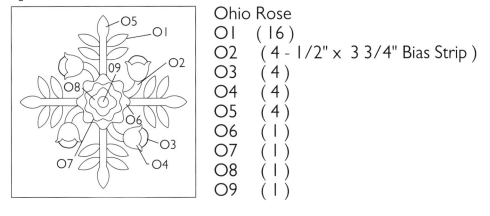

Ohio Rose
O1 (16)
O2 (4 - 1/2" x 3 3/4" Bias Strip)
O3 (4)
O4 (4)
O5 (4)
O6 (1)
O7 (1)
O8 (1)
O9 (1)

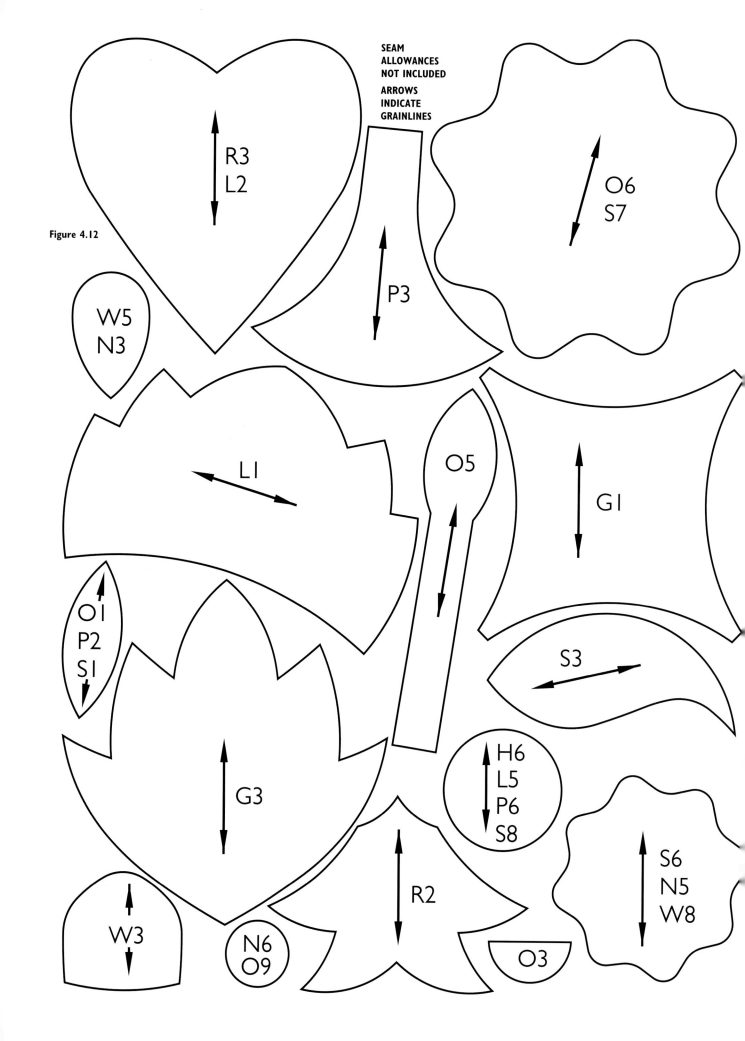

Figure 4.12

SEAM ALLOWANCES NOT INCLUDED

ARROWS INDICATE GRAINLINES

R3
L2

O6
S7

W5
N3

P3

L1

O5

G1

O1
P2
S1

S3

G3

H6
L5
P6
S8

W3

N6
O9

R2

O3

S6
N5
W8

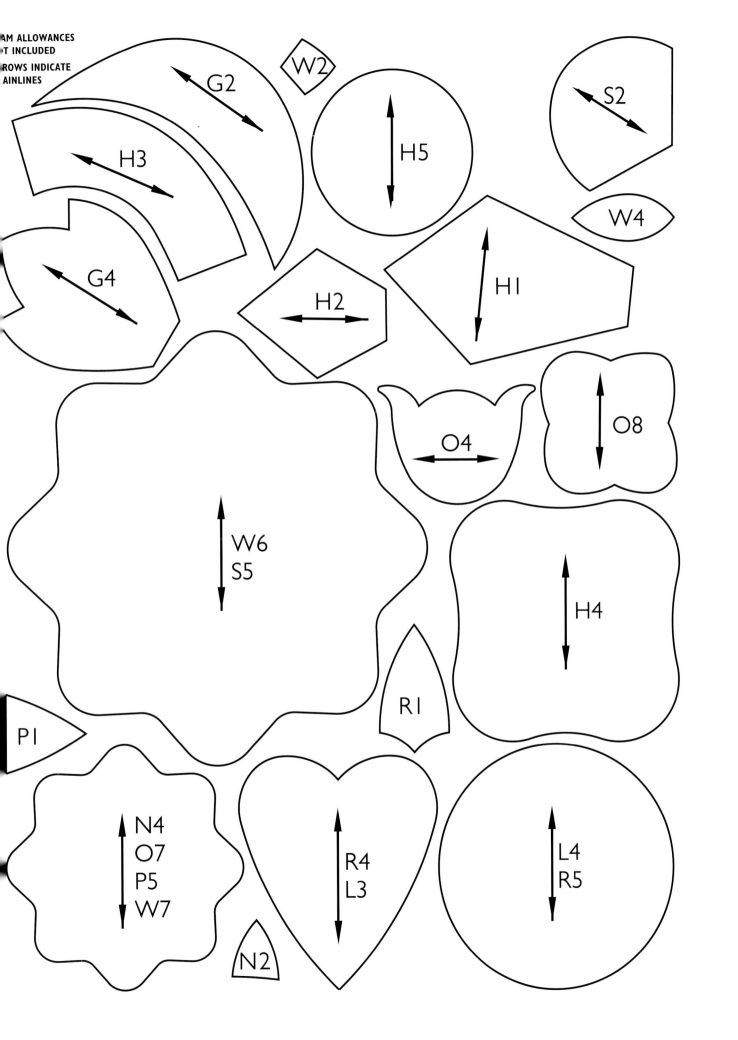

PROJECT: SAMPLER FULL-SIZE QUILT

Use this setting as a springboard for any of your 12" quilt blocks. Here the Romance of the Roses appliqué blocks alternate with plain blocks where quilting stencils can accent a plain background. Finished size is 80" × 96".

Materials

Appliqué fabrics: ¼ yard each of five to six assorted floral fabrics (include green)
Nine appliqué blocks trimmed to 12½" squares (1¼ yards)
Nine 12½" background squares for quilting in alternate blocks (1½ yards)
One 16⅞" background square cut in half on the diagonal for corner triangles
Forty-three sashing strips 12½" × 4½" (2 yards)
Twenty-eight 4½" inset squares (½ yard)
Top and side borders: cut three strips 6½" × 80½"
Bottom center border: cut a strip 6½" × 36½"
Side bottom borders: cut two strips 6½" × 40½"
Outside border material requires 2½ yards.

Method

Trim blocks to a 12½" square. Sew blocks together in vertical or horizontal strips with 4½" sashing strips between blocks. Set in squares as the spacers between remaining sashing strips. The sequence of border addition is as follows: sew sides, top, center bottom, and end with the side bottom borders.

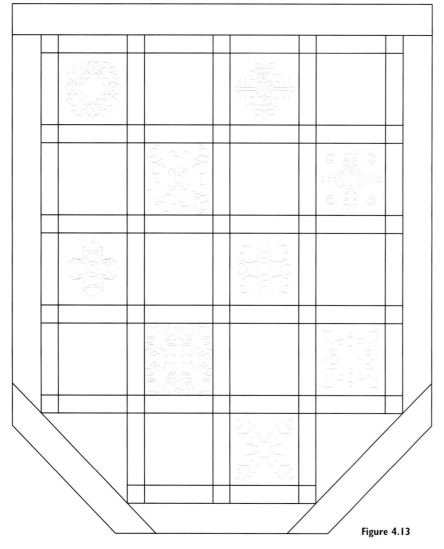

Figure 4.13

PROJECT: WALL HANGING SAMPLER QUILT

Use this setting to include all nine appliqué blocks in a sampler wall hanging. Consider choosing a favorite block and repeating it nine times, but change fabrics in each block. Consider using the templates as quilting lines in the border triangles. Finished size is 42½" × 72¼".

Materials

Nine appliqué blocks in five to
    six assorted prints: ¼ yard each
Nine foundation blocks cut 12¾" square
    (1½ yards)
Eighteen corner inset squares cut 2½"
    (¼ yard)
Twenty-six sashing strips cut 2½" × 12½"
    (¾ yard)
Five border triangles: cut a 15¼" square
    into quarter square triangles (use one
    of these to cut one other triangle)
    (½ yard)
Border corner triangles: cut a
    16⅞" square on the diagonal for
    two triangles (½ yard)

Method

Trim each appliquéd block to a 12½" square. Sew four diagonal rows of blocks and sashings together. Include the side triangles and corner triangles into the sections.

Figure 4.14

5 Foundation Piecing

A new patchwork technique has been born! But as I further examine this phenomenon, I realize it has roots in one of our oldest forms of scrap quilts — the string quilt. You must at some point in your "antique shopping" life have come across square patches stitched on old catalogs, newspapers, or even love letters! Yes, our foremothers were pretty clever to realize that a foundation made it easy to use up leftovers. Then the strips of the Log Cabin and the Pineapple quilt were seen stitched through cloth foundations. In recent times blocks have become more regulated, to the point of using the repeated shapes of our triangles, squares, and rectangles that result in unique picture blocks. Today there is even a magazine devoted to this process (see Resources).

This method of patchwork keeps evolving into many unique forms. There are many benefits that are listed below. It is a departure from the "old-fashioned" seam allowance technique, but for many it offers a lot of security to follow the line. In fact, you could call it "Sew by Number"! Most patterns today are based on a square, so I enjoyed introducing the Montana wildflowers in a diamond shape.

GUIDELINES FOR PAPER PIECING

Basic Beginning Hints

1. Begin with a simple pattern with few pieces in each block. I suggest the Prairie Thistle as a beginning block.

2. Use a light box near your machine.

3. Set your machine on a tighter stitch — as many as fifteen to twenty stitches per inch. This allows the paper to come off easier as repeated stitching occurs.

4. Use a neutral thread.

5. Start with #1 fabric placed with the wrong side against paper on the nonmarked side; glue-stick in place. Marking the template number on the reverse side of the paper also allows you to keep track of the next fabric to be stitched.

6. Marking fabric colors on paper as a guide is helpful.

7. Crease the next stitching line (which will be #2 fabric) that includes the initial fabric. Use a light box to aid in next fabric placement.

8. Align #2 fabric with right sides together, allowing the seam allowance to "eek" over the stitching mark on the paper.

9. Stitch on marked paper side, then bend both fabric and paper back to reveal stitched seam allowance. Trim an even ¼" or narrower seam allowance with the rotary cutter and see-through ruler, being careful not to cut through the paper template. Continue with each progressive number. Be certain to include outside seam allowances.

10. Do not remove paper until blocks have been set into finished project.

Advantages of Foundation Piecing

- There is accurate piecework with lines to follow for stitching.
- More difficult patterns can now be attempted.
- There are no templates to cut, draw around, or calculate.
- Bias edges are stabilized once blocks are sewn together.
- If using muslin or lightweight interfacing, there is no need to tear off the backing.
- Very little quilting is necessary, since with small piecework there is not much space.
- Multiple patterns can be made by stacking cutout paper templates, stapling them together at the top and bottom, and stitching through seam lines without any thread in the bobbin or top of sewing machine. This enables the paper to come off easier.

Disadvantages of Foundation Piecing

- It can be pesky and frustrating.
- It uses a lot more fabric; there is waste.
- The order of sewing must be followed or you will be unstitching a lot.
- It is a messy process.
- Removing the paper can be very time consuming and pesky.
- Directional fabric takes planning ahead, pinning, and peeking.
- Curves cannot be stitched, as paper does not want to bend.
- Using fabric as a foundation results in two layers to quilt through. (For a garment, of course, this could be an advantage — more warmth!)

WILDFLOWER PAPER PIECING

Try your hand and machine with each of these diamond shapes. Each diamond is cut apart into sections. The dashed lines on the figures indicate seam allowances. Remember, it's just one fabric after the next, following the numbers. I would suggest copying the patterns on a copy machine to transfer these shapes to your paper foundation. Caution: The ink will transfer to the ironing board cover, so place a disposable fabric or paper on the ironing surface. Only iron on the fabric side, as the ink can transfer to the iron also. There are many new products on the market that will tear away very easy. Some quilters like to

use very lightweight interfacing, since that does not have to be removed after stitching and is thin enough to quilt through.

My wildflowers became the border for a special Flowers on the Trail wall hanging made at the Nine Quarter Circle Ranch Quilt Retreat as a joint project with my co-teacher, Charlotte Warr Andersen. Random shades of blue fabric in 6" diamonds combine with the pieced diamonds on the border. The diamonds can also become a sampler star wall hanging based on the LeMoyne Star pattern (fig. 5.5a). Include all four diamonds, or repeat a favorite diamond four times in this design. A third option is to just let these flowers grow out of a flower pot on your kitchen window!

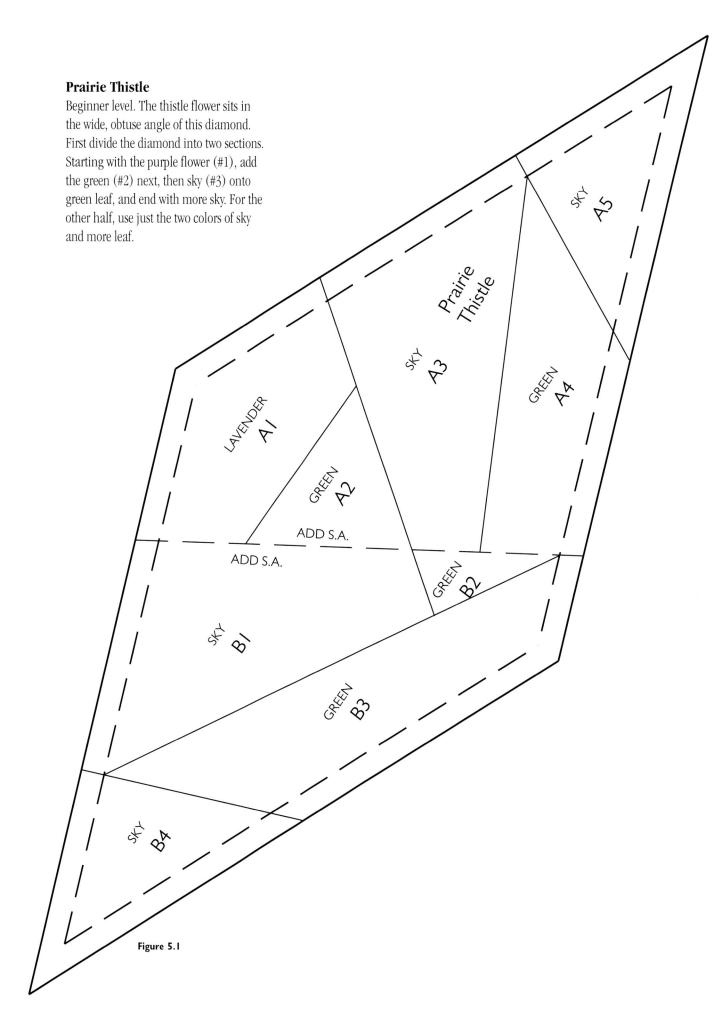

Prairie Thistle

Beginner level. The thistle flower sits in the wide, obtuse angle of this diamond. First divide the diamond into two sections. Starting with the purple flower (#1), add the green (#2) next, then sky (#3) onto green leaf, and end with more sky. For the other half, use just the two colors of sky and more leaf.

SKY A5

Prairie Thistle

SKY A3

GREEN A4

LAVENDER A1

GREEN A2

ADD S.A.

ADD S.A.

GREEN B2

SKY B1

GREEN B3

SKY B4

Figure 5.1

Sticky Geranium

Intermediate level. Five petals form this geranium surrounded by sky and a single stem. A wavy or geometric striped fabric works well with this design. Cut the paper pattern apart on all of the slash lines. Stitch the flower petals one section at a time, keeping the paper on to align the crossover symbols. Stitch three sections of the geranium together, then stitch two sections together so these can be pinned and completed by sewing from the center, backstitching at the quarter-inch center point. Add the surrounding sky pieces, #4 and #7. The stem can be stitched with a continuous bias or pieced in three sections. A curved stem is an option also.

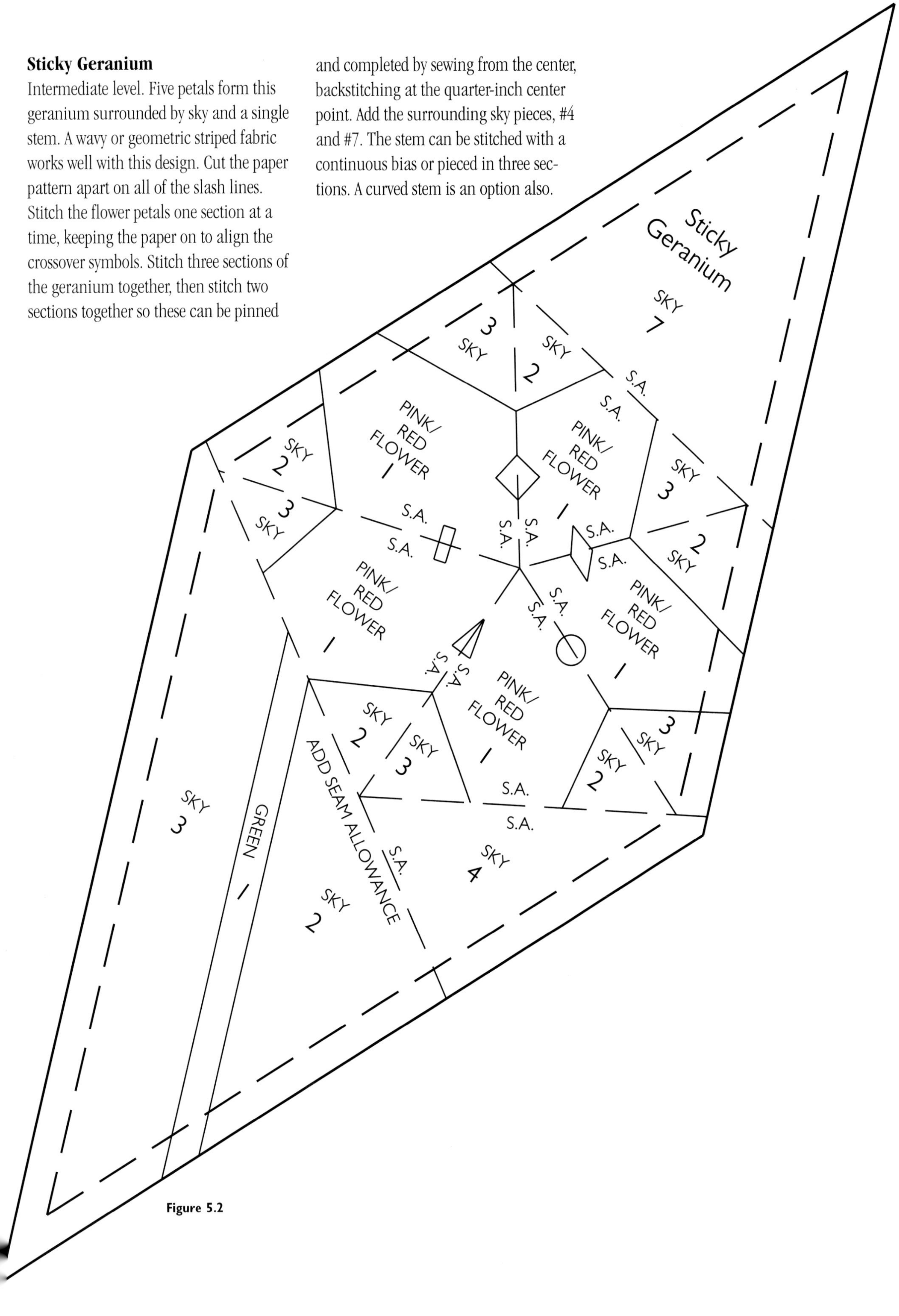

Sticky Geranium

SKY 7

SKY 3

SKY 2

SKY 2

S.A.

S.A.

PINK/ RED FLOWER

PINK/ RED FLOWER

SKY 3

SKY 2

SKY 3

SKY 2

PINK/ RED FLOWER

S.A.

S.A.

S.A.

S.A.

S.A.

PINK/ RED FLOWER

S.A.

S.A.

PINK/ RED FLOWER

SKY 2

SKY 3

SKY 3

SKY 2

S.A.

S.A.

S.A.

ADD SEAM ALLOWANCE

S.A.

SKY 4

SKY 3

GREEN

SKY 2

Figure 5.2

Wild Lupine

Intermediate level. Divide the diamond in half through the long, acute angles. Choose three sets of colors for each flower bud, to be stitched opposite each other next to the stem. The last colors to be added are at the top. Be certain to trim the seam allowance very narrow for #8 and #9 stem when first adding the green fabric, but add a complete ¼" seam allowance on the stem outside for these two triangles to then be sewn together.

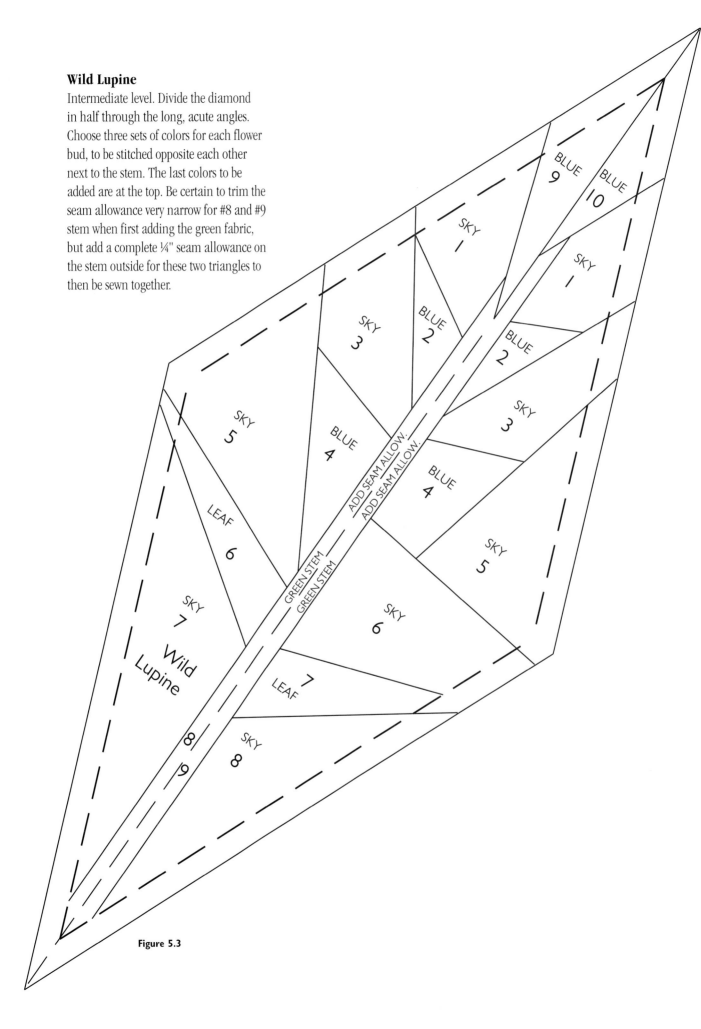

Figure 5.3

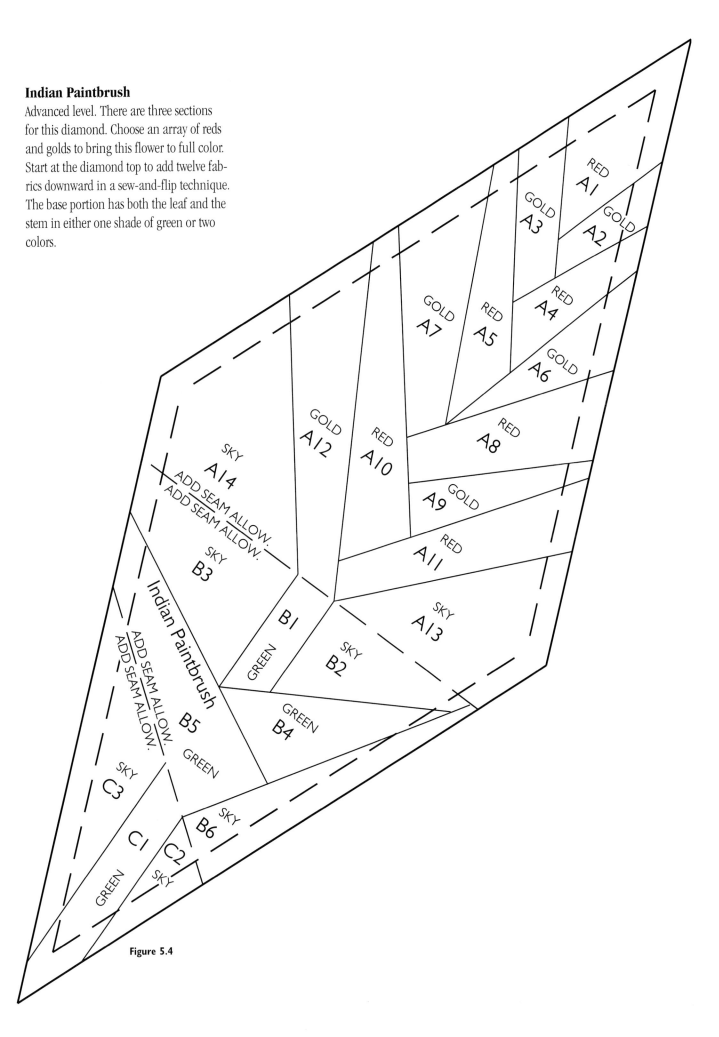

Indian Paintbrush

Advanced level. There are three sections for this diamond. Choose an array of reds and golds to bring this flower to full color. Start at the diamond top to add twelve fabrics downward in a sew-and-flip technique. The base portion has both the leaf and the stem in either one shade of green or two colors.

RED A1

GOLD A3

GOLD A2

GOLD A7

RED A5

RED A4

GOLD A6

GOLD A12

RED A10

RED A8

SKY A14

ADD SEAM ALLOW.
ADD SEAM ALLOW.

A9 GOLD

RED A11

SKY B3

B1

SKY A13

GREEN

SKY B2

Indian Paintbrush

ADD SEAM ALLOW.
ADD SEAM ALLOW.

B5

GREEN B4

GREEN

SKY C3

SKY B6

C1

C2

GREEN

SKY

Figure 5.4

PROJECT: DIAMOND STAR SAMPLER

The classic LeMoyne Star fills four of its diamonds with wildflowers that point outward. Another option would be to repeat one diamond four times. Each time the alternate diamonds are cut out in a single fabric. A 20½" block with borders makes a 30" square.

Materials

½ yard of print fabric for diamonds and border sashing
½ yard of dark print fabric for background and sashing
⅛ yard of accent sashing fabric
Small amounts of flower fabric and sky blue for diamond background
1 yard of backing fabric and 32" square of batting

20 ½"
Sqr.

Figure 5.5a

Method

1. Cut out a 4¾" × 32" print fabric rectangle and introduce a 45° angle to cut the first acute angle. Then, maintaining a parallel, cut apart every 4¾" to yield four diamonds (fig. 5.5b).

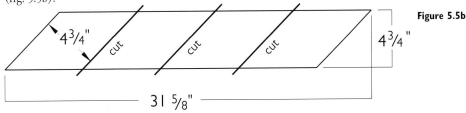

4³/₄"
cut
cut
cut
4³/₄"

31 ⁵/₈"

Figure 5.5b

2. Stitch four different wildflower diamonds (or stitch the same diamond four times). When completed, sew the star together in sets of two. Backstitch each at the inside right angles, leaving a free-floating seam. Sew two sets together to have four and four diamonds. Keep the seam allowance going in the same concentric direction on the backside. Sew the two halves together by alternating the intersection seams in opposite directions. Once sewn, release a few of the initial stitches so a twirl occurs at the intersection (fig. 5.5c).

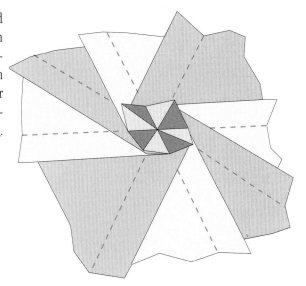

Figure 5.5c

3. Cut apart the 9¾" square on the diagonal for the triangle setting pieces. Cut four 6½" corner squares (fig. 5.5d).

Figure 5.5d

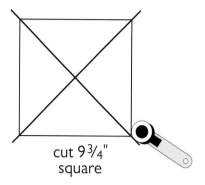

cut 4

cut 6¹/2"
square

cut 9³/4"
square

4. Sew the triangles into two diamond points four times. Align the diamond end first and then stitch inward to the ¼" seam, backstitching in place. Complete by adding the squares on each corner. Stitch only up to the ¼" seam, backstitch again. Sew from the inside right angle, outward each time. (See Chapter 3, figs. 3.23d–h.)

5. Border additions:

First set of borders: Cut two accent fabrics 1½" × 21". Cut two accent fabrics 1½" × 23½".

Second set of borders: Cut two print fabrics 2" × 23". Cut two print fabrics 2" × 26".

Third set of borders: Cut two dark fabrics 2½" × 26". Cut two dark fabrics 2½" × 31".

6. Layer Star Block with batting and backing, and hand quilt. I quilted around some of the diamond flowers and did straight, radiating lines from the corner squares. Bind with a continuous bias.

Figure 5.6

6 Stitch by Stitch

Yard by yard, life can be hard, but inch by inch, it's a cinch. I relate this to quiltmaking. Gazing on a pretty quilt and then pondering how to make it can be intimidating, an overwhelming project. But with a basic sewing background and patchwork know-how you can be a quilter. So stitch by stitch, I present two quilt projects that start at the beginning and proceed step by step toward completion. Then I'll show you two new methods of using the gridded freezer paper — strip picture piecing and curved designs.

Creating quilting programs for television is fun. The show that featured these quilts was easy to name and assemble once Penny Wortman told me the name of her quilt, Corn and Beans. The seasons were in my mind as I planned a spring show with Montana wildflowers. So what comes next? Summertime, with corn growing in the fields. Corn needs sunshine, so my Sunface fit right in, and Cornfields Forever presented the gently rolling fields in curved patchwork. Of course the pièce de résistance, my great-grandmother's recipe for dried corn, ended that particular show.

Another group endeavor that has special meaning is the Housing Project quilts. For the last fourteen years I have taught the same group of ladies at a lodge called Freedom Escape in Weaverville, North Carolina. For a teacher, this is the ultimate opportunity to shape patchwork lives — we are marooned for a week with only our cloth and sewing machines! Partake in one of our latest projects, geared for a group quilt. You will want this house quilt for yourself and all of your friends. So start planning, cutting, and stitching.

PROJECT: CORN AND BEANS QUILT

It's scrappy. It's traditional. It's bright. It's full of quilting. It sparks. What more could you want in a quilt? I am proud to feature this quilt by Penelope Ratzlaff Wortman. She was in one of my earliest lap quilting classes and continues to use that method for her full-sized quilts. They gather many ribbons at our local shows. She is a perfectionist and a true quilter devoted to the cloth. She continues to share her work on my television programs and in my books. Thanks, Penny! Finished size is 65" × 85".

Materials
3½ yards of light/background fabric
Scraps/remnants of twelve different red calicoes
Scraps/remnants of mixed calicoes (include green for beans and yellow for corn)
5 yards of backing fabric
30" square of fabric for binding

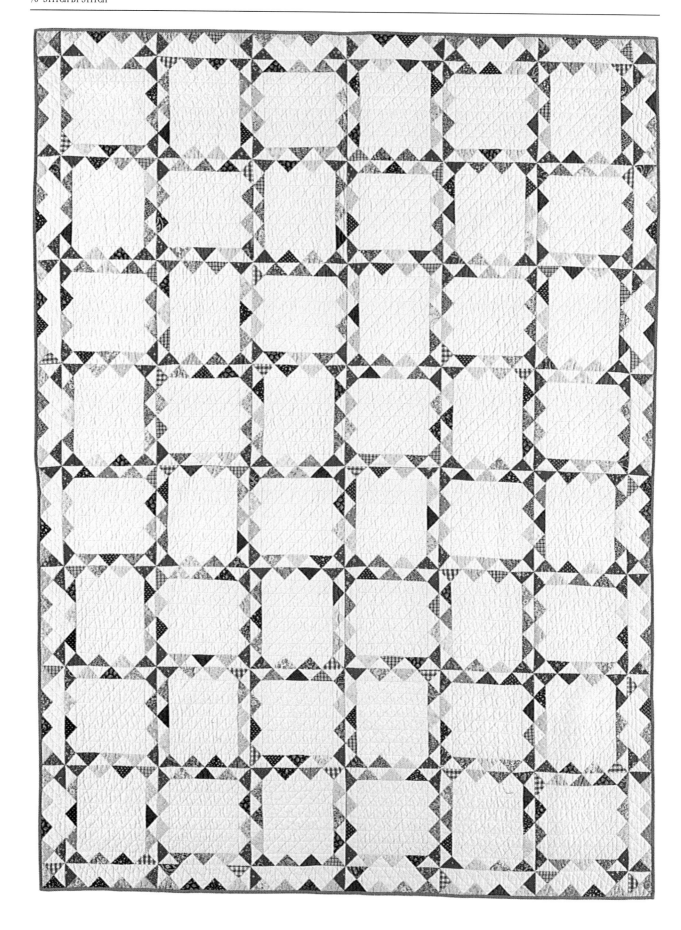

Cutting

Cut forty-eight 8" squares of light/background fabric.

Align light/background fabric with twelve different red calicoes and cut 3¾" squares.

Cut 120 3¾" squares of mixed calico and light/background fabric. Cut these squares apart on the diagonal both ways (see figs. 6.1a–d).

Border Cuts

Cut fourteen A and fourteen B templates from light/background fabric.

Cut thirty 3¾" squares of light/background fabric, thirty squares of mixed calico fabric, and fifteen squares of red calico fabric. Cut these apart on the diagonal both ways (see figs. 6.1a–d).

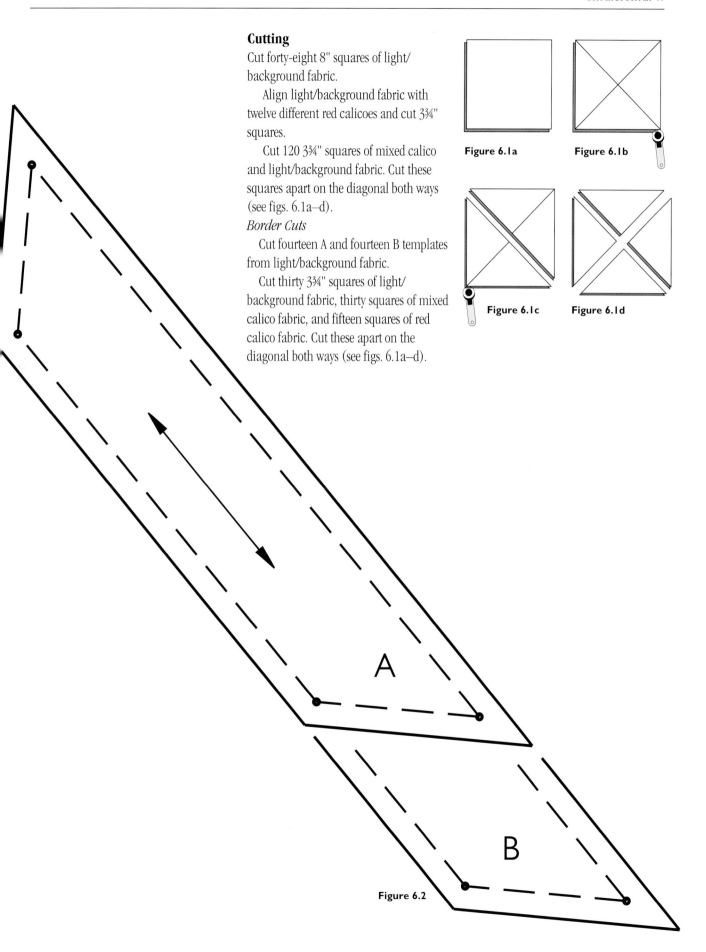

Figure 6.1a   Figure 6.1b

Figure 6.1c   Figure 6.1d

A

B

Figure 6.2

Method

1. Stitch forty-eight blocks, adding the triangles onto each side. Sew five triangles to each side of the 8" square. Alternate color with light triangles. Follow the schematic (fig. 6.3) so that the dark and light sides of the triangles are turned properly. Note that two sides have the dark triangles sewn on the center square and light triangles sewn on the other two sides.

Figure 6.3

2. Draw a diagonal line both ways across the light and red combination of 3¾" squares. Machine stitch a ¼" seam on either side of one diagonal; cut apart on both diagonal lines (see figs. 6.4a–c). Stitch these red/light combinations on each corner. Mix these combinations for a scrappy look.

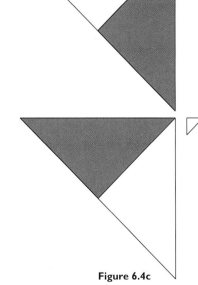

Figure 6.4a

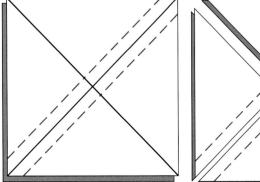

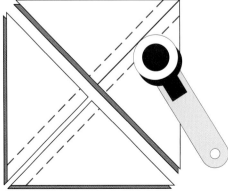

Figure 6.4b

Figure 6.4c

3. Sew blocks together by alternating blocks a quarter turn, three blocks across and four blocks down. This quilt was lap quilted in four sections with the borders attached (fig. 6.5).

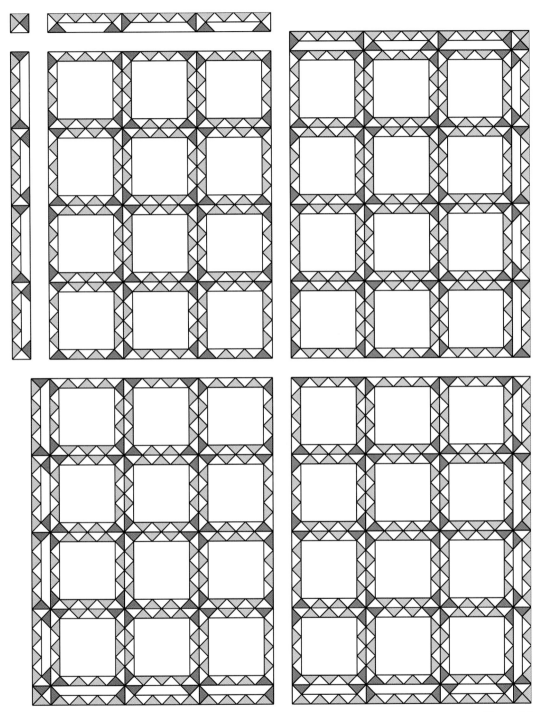

Figure 6.5

4. Sew borders together, alternating the A and B templates, and attach to the perimeter of each of the four panels.

5. Cut batting and backing into the proper sizes (33" × 43") for basting the four sections together. Quilt around each calico triangle and diagonal crosshatch in the light center squares. Leave the inside connecting seams unquilted for at least 1". You can even

leave a floating, loose quilting thread to rethread and quilt once the connection of panels is complete. Trim excess batting and backing to be even with the front.

6. The lap quilting connection is made by pinning the batting and backing to the back and aligning the raw edges of the front two panels. Pin in place and machine stitch together. Unpin the back, and with the partial quilt on a flat surface, trim any excess batting so sections of batting butt up next to each other, without any lumpy sections. Let one edge of the backing rest flat, and turn under a ¼" seam allowance on the other side. Baste this in place and then connect with a tiny, hidden appliqué stitch. Be careful not to go through to the frontside. After each of the two panels are connected, sew these together and perform the same lap quilting connection on the backside. Take care of any dangling threads. Trim excess batting and backing around the quilt outside; baste the raw edges together.

7. Bind the quilt with a continuous bias cut 2½" wide.

HOUSING PROJECT QUILTS

What unique houses, each one representing a quilting friend. It's true my smoke looks somewhat like Santa's boot stuck in the chimney, and my mountains stop short, but, hey, this is a folk quilt. The pattern was inspired by a Checkerboard House quilt from *American Patchwork and Quilting* magazine, designer Mary Tendall, and Connie Tesene of Country Threads. Quilted by Shirley Henion and yours truly.

Project: Housing Project I
Finished size is 60" × 86½".

Materials
Lots of scrap fabric for variety in each house
Remnants of various greens for the folded trees; brown for tree trunks
1 yard of green fabric
2 yards of sky blue fabric
5 yards for backing and binding

Cutting
Directions are for cutting one 8" block house (see fig. 6.8). Multiply each template times the number of houses desired for your special wall hanging or quilt.
#1 Window: cut a 2½" square.
#2 House: cut a 2½" × 1½" rectangle.
#3 House: cut a 1½" × 3½" rectangle.
#4 House: cut two rectangles 2" × 3½".
#5 Door: cut a 3½" × 2½" rectangle.
#6 House: cut a 1½" × 8½" rectangle.
#7 Sky: cut a 2⅞" square and then cut apart on the diagonal. Save extra for another house.
#8 Chimney: cut a 2½" × 4⅞" rectangle with a 45° angle cut off the bottom edge for the proper diagonal (see fig. 3.14 in Chapter 3).
#9 Roof: cut a 9¼" square on the diagonal both ways to yield three extra roof triangles. Save extra for three other houses.

Groupie Guidelines

HOUSING PROJECT I

Each quilter made her own house times the number in the group. Yes, we gave ourselves a whole year to complete our houses and then exchanged, so we each had twenty-two different houses. Each quilter went out of her way to personalize her house—tiny yo-yos for flowers, curtains in the windows, special trees, and button accents. You can really get a mass assembly line going when you are repeating the same block many times with the same accents. (Fig 6.6)

HOUSING PROJECT II

The second quilt, which will be used as a twin to the first house quilt, has an entirely different setting based on the maple leaf pattern. It could be called a tree house. Students came to class with enough light and dark fabric to cut out all eleven house templates times the number of students—fifteen in this instance. Each house required a rectangle 12" × 14", so 1⅔ yards of light and dark fabric were needed to cut out the fifteen templates. Each house was pinned together in a set. Each person kept one set of her own light and dark, but received fourteen new sets of light and dark. The fun began as each house was stitched together in a different manner. I choose to keep every piece of fabric different and contrast the light and dark roof with the sky and contrast the window/door with the house background. To add zip I set each house with half-square green and blue triangles accented with a stem. (Fig 6.7)

Figure 6.6

#10 Sky: cut a 4⅞" square and then cut apart on the diagonal. Save extra for another house.

Below each house block is a 2" × 8" (cut 2½" × 8½") green panel with random dark appliqué pathways (template B). This elongates the house rectangle 8" × 10".

Tree Panel: Between the house blocks is an 8" × 10" tree block using the Folded Flying Geese technique (see Chapter 1). The following measurements are for one block; multiply any template times the number of blocks desired.

Figure 6.7

Method

1. A1: cut a ¾" × 4½" sky rectangle.

2. A2: cut two 2½" sky squares and one (A3) 2½" × 4½" tree rectangle to fold into seam.

3. A4: cut a 3½" × 4½" sky rectangle and appliqué a 1" × 3½" tree trunk.

4. B1: cut two 2" × 2½" sky rectangles and one (B2) 2½" × 2" tree rectangle to fold into seam.

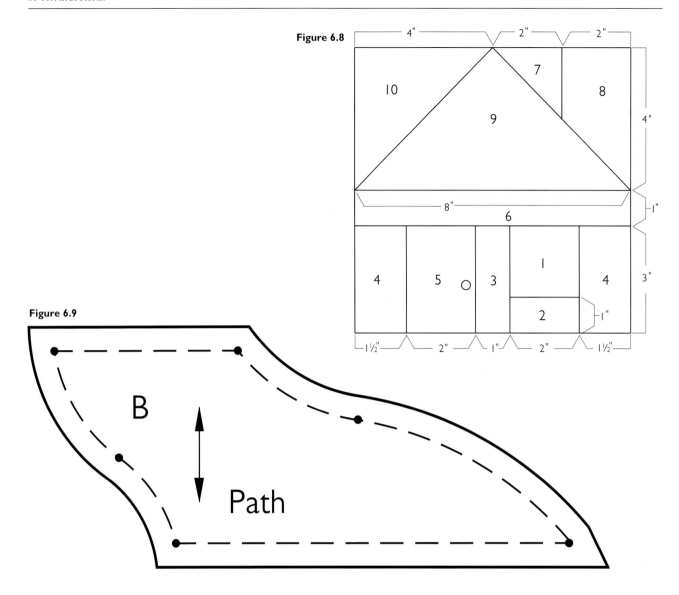

Figure 6.8

Figure 6.9

B

Path

5. B3: cut a 4½" × 5¼" sky rectangle and appliqué a 1¼" × 5¼" tree trunk.

6. AB4: cut a 3½" × 6½" tree to fold into connecting seam. (See fig. 6.10a.)

The bottom gridded panel can be made with a 3¾" × 8" Grid Grip® panel. Trace a centered 1"-wide tree trunk with curved lines using a flexible drafting tool. Cut these five templates out and press onto sky, tree trunk, and grass fabric adding a ¼" seam allowance on all sides. Remove Grid Grip® before sewing curves. Sew together according to the number sequence (fig. 6.10b).

Top Sky Panel. This is a 2½" × 40½" panel stitched above each row of connected houses. The smoke (template A) is appliquéd in position above the chimney before the seam connection.

Border Blocks. This is a 10" × 12" rectangle. Follow the suggested lines in fig. 6.12 for drawing the curved lines with a flexible drafting tool. If using Grid Grip® or template plastic, cut out a mirror image for each side by placing either the wrong or right sides of two fabrics together.

Bottom Grass Panel. Cut a 3" × 60½" grass panel to be sewn on the quilt bottom.

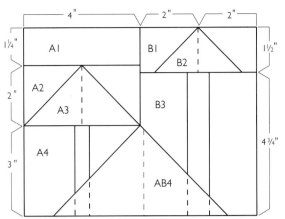

Figure 6.10a

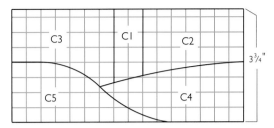

Figure 6.10b

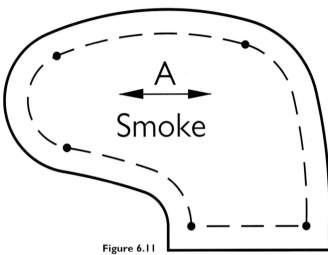

A

Smoke

Figure 6.11

Figure 6.12

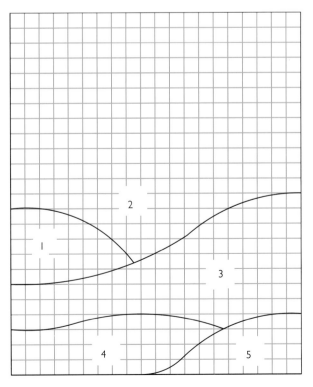

Project: Housing Project II

The tree house rendition uses twenty-eight scrap, pieced houses with half-square triangle and stem accents. Finished size is 60" × 86½". (See fig. 6.7.)

Materials
2½ yards of sky blue fabric
Scraps of green for Folded Flying Geese and triangles
Brown for tree trunks
5 yards for backing and binding (30" square)

Cutting
Cut twenty-eight 4½" sky squares.
Align fourteen sky squares with different greens to cut 9¾" squares.
Cut twenty-eight dark stems (template C); vary the direction, for fun!

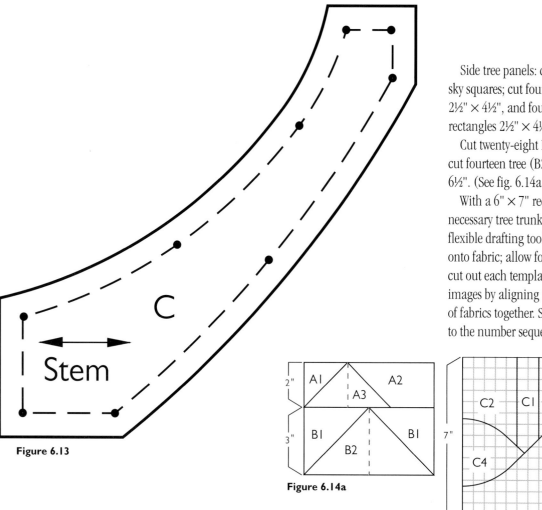

Figure 6.13

Side tree panels: cut fourteen A1 2½" sky squares; cut fourteen A2 sky rectangles 2½" × 4½", and fourteen tree (A3) rectangles 2½" × 4½".

Cut twenty-eight B1 3½" sky squares; cut fourteen tree (B2) rectangles 3½" × 6½". (See fig. 6.14a.)

With a 6" × 7" rectangle, draw the necessary tree trunk and soft curves with a flexible drafting tool. Cut apart and press onto fabric; allow for seam allowances to cut out each template. Create mirror images by aligning the right or wrong side of fabrics together. Sew together according to the number sequence (fig. 6.14b).

Figure 6.14a

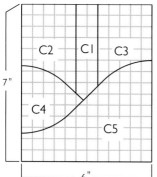

Figure 6.14b

Method

1. Stitch the twenty-eight scrap houses.

2. With the nine ¾" squares aligned, draw diagonal lines and quarter section lines. Sew a quarter-inch on either side of the diagonal lines. Cut apart on quarter-square lines and diagonal lines (fig. 6.15). Press seam allowances and trim dog ears.

3. Place half-square triangles to the side and base of houses, mixing up colors and pattern for balance. Appliqué a stem on the square. Sew the half-square triangles together in pairs. Stitch a pair to each house. Sew the stem square onto the other triangle pairs. Complete the block with the other panel.

4. Sew vertical rows of five houses each. Then sew the seven rows together to complete the top. Add the side tree panels of 6" × 12" along each side. Add a base panel 3½" × 60½". (See fig. 6.7.)

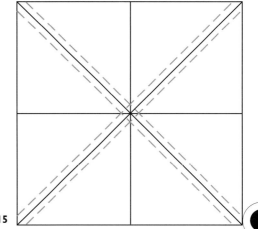

Figure 6.15

PROJECT: CORNFIELDS FOREVER

The Cornfields Forever wall hanging features four of the Cornfields 8" blocks, two sets of mirror-image blocks. There is a New England expression that I always think of when designing curves: "A straight line is a line of duty, but a curved line is a line of beauty." Most of our patchwork is sewing straight lines, so it is always a new twist to introduce curved lines. I use a flexible drafting tool to draw these lines, keeping the curve gentle and not too extreme. Drafting, cutting, and pressing can be done on Grid Grip®, but not the machine stitching, as paper will not bend at the machine. Templates are offered here with the seam allowance included. Note the A, B, and C sections (fig. 6.17).

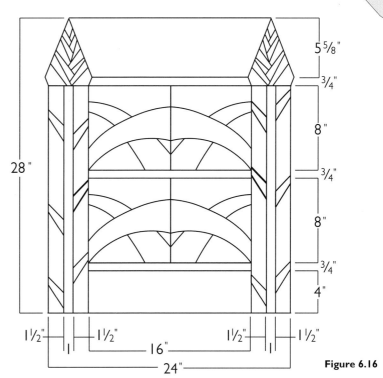

Figure 6.16

Figure 6.17

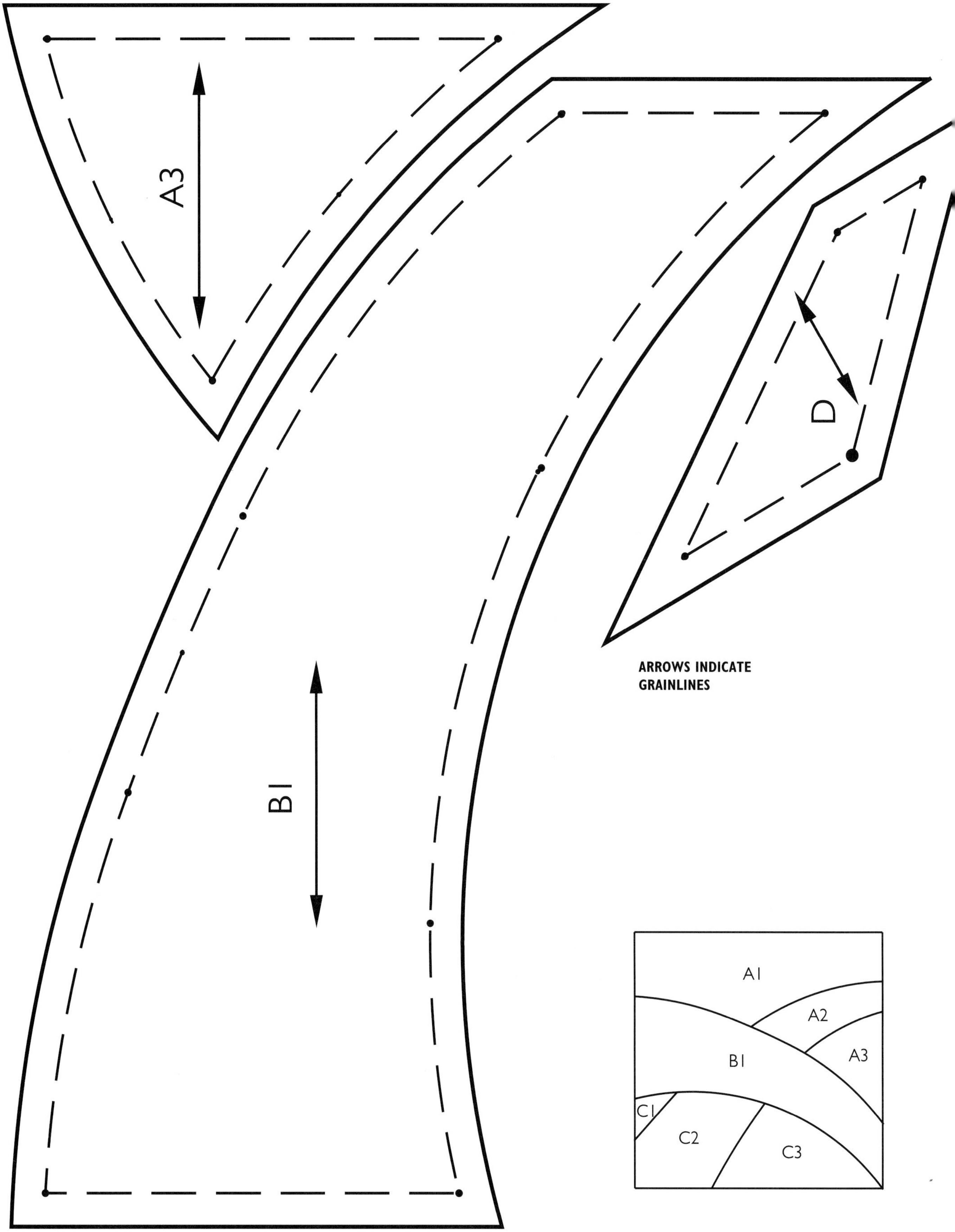

A3

D

B1

ARROWS INDICATE
GRAINLINES

A1

A2

A3

B1

C1

C2

C3

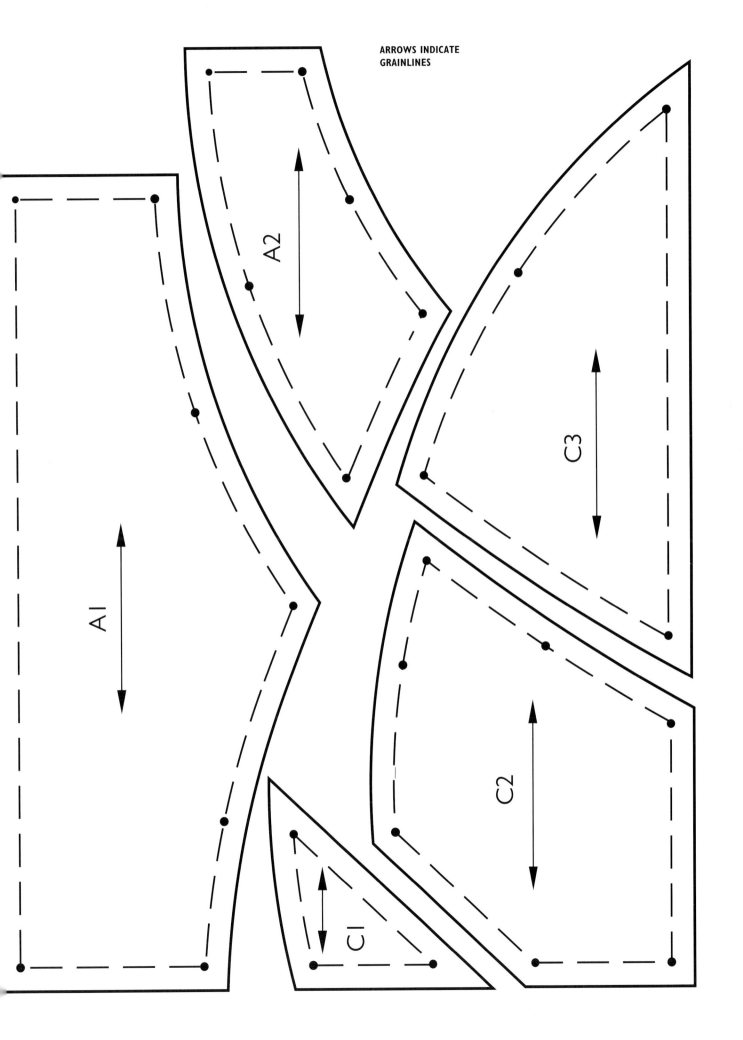

ARROWS INDICATE
GRAINLINES

A2

C3

A1

C2

C1

Setting options are endless, depending on how the blocks are cut out. Either all fabrics go in the same direction or are cut out in duplicate with the wrong or right sides of fabrics together. Play with these possibilities (see fig. 6.18). The corn tassel tops of the cornstalks are part of the Indian Paintbrush paper piecing diamond (see Wildflower Paper Piecing in Chapter 5 for pattern). Finished size is 24" × 28".

Figure 6.18

Materials

½ yard of background fabric
¼ yard of sky fabric
Remnants of corn, river, and grass fabric
Gold, corn-colored fabric
⅔ yard of backing fabric

Cutting

Cut two sets of mirror-image templates for all seven A, B, and C figures. A1 uses the same sky fabric; A3, C1, and C3 use the same green fabric; A2 and C2 use the same water fabric; B1 uses four different shades of cornfields.

Cut three light bands 1¼" × 16½" to stitch on either side of blocks.

Cut bottom border, 4½" × 16½".

Cut top border, 5⅞" × 16½".

Cut four outside background strips 2" × 22".

Cut two green stalks 1½" × 22".

Cut six pairs of mirror-image template D.

Method

1. Stitch four Cornfields blocks together, following the number sequence.

2. Make two copies of the top portion of the Indian Paintbrush. Sew on the paper to complete the corn tassels, using gold, red, orange, and green.

3. Sew the two rows together and stitch the narrow panels on either side. Add the bottom panel. Appliqué the D template onto the background strips. Sew these on either side of the green stalk. Stitch to the center portion.

4. Add the partial Indian Paintbrush on top. Sew on the top border and then appliqué the inside angle onto this background.

5. Quilt as desired, either by machine, by hand, or a combination of both.

STRIP PICTURE PIECING: SUNFACE

Any design can be transposed into cloth via strips, using Grid Grip®. Using an enlarging machine, capture the preferred enlarged size for any design. When I copied the Sunface (inspired by a graphic by M. Martiros), even the enlargements intrigued me, so I used those as panels behind the colorful face.

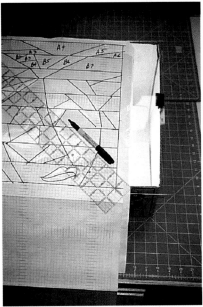

1. Enlarge design to desired size. Decide if design should be separated by horizontal or vertical strips.

2. Place Grid Grip® on top of the design, using a light box or a sunny sliding glass door. Divide the paper into rows, either symmetrical or uneven, to accommodate the lines underneath. Where there are curved lines, straighten them out in between the long pieced rows. For any directional design, such as letters, transfer from the reverse of the design.

3. Code the rows, A, B, etc., and number the sequence of piecing, starting at the top. Also mark any fabric codes to indicate where colors change.

4. Cut out fabric ½" wider than the strips. Cut templates apart and press onto the cloth strips, keeping a ¼" seam allowance on either side. Align grid with straight of grain of strips. Use the paper edge as a sewing guide, pinning and peeking before you sew. Pull off paper when sewing rows together, after using the paper as a guide to pin before sewing.

5. Store templates if you want to reuse them.

RECIPE: DRIED CORN À LA "GAGA"

As a girl I was always intrigued by a special summertime kitchen exercise my mother performed at the peak corn-on-the-cob season. We never reaped the benefit of this process, however, until Thanksgiving or Christmas. This recipe had been passed on to her from her grandmother, Charlotte Bradshaw Sayler of Portage, Ohio. Now, through the generations, just like quilting, I pass it on to you.

Ingredients

Several dozen ears of sweet corn — not field corn, but good corn on the cob. The yield depends on the size of the corn. Every year I record how much I get from the amount cooked. It is about 1 cup of corn for every dozen ears — sometimes a bit more.

Method

Shuck each ear of sweet corn, removing as much silk and little "varmints" at the narrow end as possible. Blanch the ears of corn in boiling water for 3 minutes, no longer. After cooling the ears, cut the corn from the cob onto cookies sheets. Scrape each cob for excess. Place in 250° oven. Stir the corn around as it dries out slowly; the outside will dry faster. Drying will take many hours. (Mother used to stay up into the wee hours for this, but we have now figured out it's easier to turn the oven off and turn it on again in the morning.) Don't scorch the corn. It will be a golden tan when done and smell like roasted corn.

Store in plastic bags in the freezer. During the holidays, remove 1 cup, cover with water, soak for 30 minutes, then simmer for 15 to 20 minutes, slowly. Add salt and pepper to taste, 1 teaspoon of butter, ¼ cup of cream, and a pinch of sugar. Yum-Yum!

7 A Hands-on Holiday

For many, the holidays culminate as the peak patchwork time of the year. This is a time to put your creative hands to work for the pleasure of giving from the heart. Make any of the following projects that feature new twists and turns of fabric. It's the time to decorate with special fabric touches, such as the Woolen Christmas Wreath. It's a time to make particular gifts for new members of the family, especially a Baby Bonesteel Quilt. It's a time to dress up with new quilting clothes, such as the Greek Shepherd's Coat with an extra special Bow Tie twist. How do we carry all of this? The Quilter's Tote-All, of course.

PROJECT: WOOLEN CHRISTMAS WREATH

Sometimes the best quilting tips are passed on by word of mouth. Corinne Meyer from Tennessee was sporting a unique vest, so I inquired as to the method of those folded triangles. Of course, in exchange, I showed her the Folded Flying Geese. Selecting the proper colors results in a unique wreath with a red bow accent at the top. See if you can find some fun ways to include this method in your quilts. Recycled wool is used as the fabric here, but cotton will work just as well. Finished size is 15" square.

Figure 7.1

Materials and Cutting

Cut twelve 5" background fabric squares.

Cut two 5" red fabric squares.

Cut twenty-two 5" assorted green fabric squares.

Fabric rectangle 16" × 4" for a tube for hanging the wreath

Narrow wooden lattice strip, 1½" × 15"

Method

1. Fold all the 5" squares on the diagonal and press lightly (fig. 7.2). For woolen squares, place a small amount of cedar chips as a moth repellent inside each triangle fold.

Pin in place. Interlock four triangles with the bias (folded) edges directed toward the inside (fig. 7.3).

2. Continue this interlock for all nine sections. Baste each square together and position as a basic nine patch, noting the red bow at the top center (see fig. 7.1).

3) Connect each square by a decorative machine stitch or a simple zigzag stitch or a hand buttonhole stitch with yarn. Continue the same decorative stitching around the outside of the square.

4) Stitch the 4"-wide rectangle into a tube, fold in each end, and hand stitch to the top backside. Insert wooden lattice.

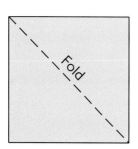

Figure 7.2

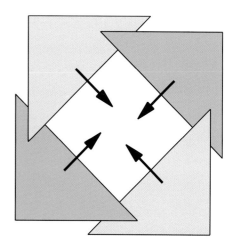

Figure 7.3

PROJECT: BABY BONESTEEL QUILT

A wonderful addition to any layette is this reversible, novel baby quilt using thirty-two enclosed squares, made block by block. Finished size is 38½" × 48".

Materials and Cutting

Cut sixty-four 5½" squares from 1½ yards baby print fabric.
Cut sixty-four 5½" squares from 1½ yards contrasting fabric (stripes, checks, plaids, etc.).
Thirty-two squares of lightweight batting cut 7" square

Method

1. Sew thirty-two four patch blocks with two prints and two contrasting squares (fig. 7.4). Release the back center seam allowance to create a flat, twirled intersection. Place the 7" square of batting diagonally on the backside and secure with two pins on the block frontside or machine baste the batting to the fabric on all four corners (fig. 7.5).

2. Fold the four patch in half with the right sides together, and machine stitch the side seams (fig. 7.6).

3. Open the sewn block and fold, with the new seam in the center to realign the raw edges, and stitch the block closed, except for a 2" opening. Note that the stitching includes the center intersection (figs. 7.7a–c). Turn the block inside out. Secure the batting in all four corners, and slip stitch the opening closed. Remove any pins or basting stitches.

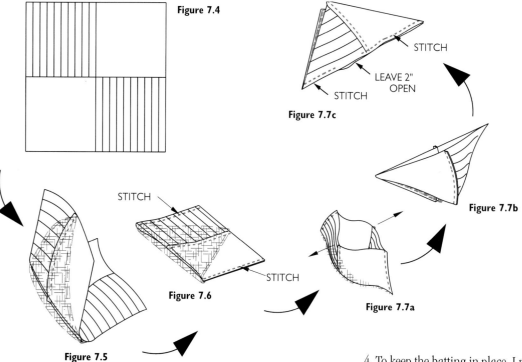

Figure 7.4

STITCH

LEAVE 2"
OPEN

STITCH

Figure 7.7c

Figure 7.7b

STITCH

STITCH

Figure 7.6

Figure 7.7a

Figure 7.5

4. To keep the batting in place, I machine quilted a 4" circle in the center of each square.

5. Arrange the blocks in a pleasing setting to balance color and design. There will be eight diagonal rows to be whip stitched together: two rows of seven blocks, two rows of five blocks, two rows of three blocks, and two single blocks at each opposite corner. Attach blocks together with a hand whip stitch or a machine zigzag or decorative stitch. The folded edges are on the bias, so do not pull or tug when stitching. The edge-stitch foot on my sewing machine has a dropped bar that aids in butting up each of these folds for sewing.

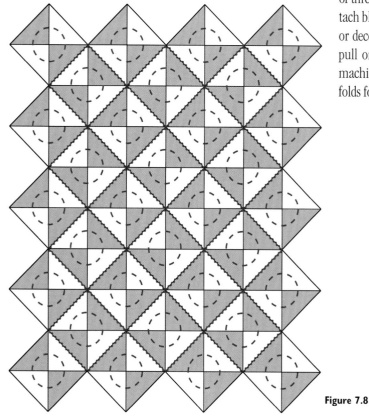

Figure 7.8

PROJECT: GREEK SHEPHERD'S COAT

A decorative, warm coat sporting a clever continuous Bow Tie technique. Consider any of your favorite patchwork designs to fill in this 12"-wide area. The special character of this coat is that each section is competed without any raw edges to be connected with a button-hole stitch.

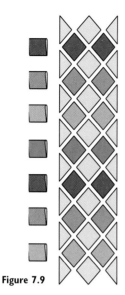

Figure 7.9

Finished size is 24" wide × 37" long, which fits medium to large sizes. For smaller sizes, reduce the mitered border and sleeve proportions.

Materials and Cutting

Cut thirty-two 3½" background squares.

Cut sixty-four background triangles by first cutting sixteen 5½" squares and then cutting these apart on the diagonal in each direction.

Cut twenty-eight sets of Bow Tie fabrics. Cut three for each set 3½" (some sets could be repeated).

Cut 6⅔ yards of 4"-wide border fabric to sew on the outside of Bow Tie panels.

¾ yard of accent fabric for sleeves and hood, such as melton wool, denim, polar fleece, or corduroy

2 yards of thin cotton batting

2¼ yards of lining fabric

Yarn for buttonhole connection stitches

5 decorative buttons

Method

1. Complete four Bow Tie panels as follows:

First: Lay out the order for each row to balance design and color. Fold the third Bow Tie square to correspond with the other squares into rectangles (fig. 7.9).

Second: Starting at one end, sew a Folded Bow Tie block. Place the extra folded rectangle, with the short sides, between the right sides of contrasting squares and machine stitch them together. Then sew the other short side of the folded rectangle between the remaining squares, switching colors (fig. 7.10a). There is now a bridge between the folded rectangle. Open that rectangle and secure in between the four patch and sew across the long seam, staggering the seam allowance on each side (figs. 7.10b and c). Release the seam allowance on the backside and press for a softer intersection and to reveal a 6½" Bow Tie block (fig. 7.10d).

Third: Sew triangles to each of the Bow Tie squares, including the Bow Tie block just completed (fig. 7.11).

Figure 7.10a

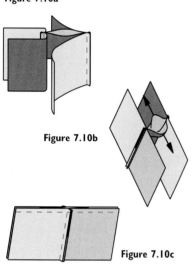

Figure 7.10b

Figure 7.10c

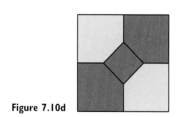

Figure 7.10d

Figure 7.11

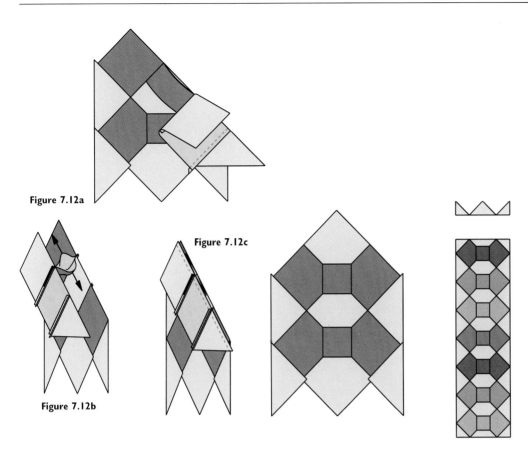

Figure 7.12a

Figure 7.12c

Figure 7.12b

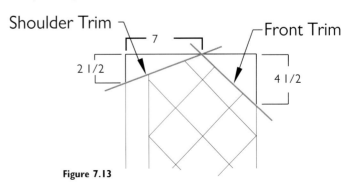

Figure 7.12d

Fourth: Now you are ready to continue adding continuous Bow Tie blocks. For the next Bow Tie, sew the folded rectangle in between contrasting right angle squares. Now, pin the other short end of the rectangle in between the companion color square and against a background fabric and stitch in place. Sew this other end of the rectangle into the contrasting squares (fig. 7.12a). Opening up the rectangle, pin it between the four patch block and stitch the long seam, staggering the center seams. For a softer back intersection, release the original seams so that all seams go in a concentric direction (fig. 7.12b). (See Chapter 5, fig. 5.5c). This time the outside setting triangles are included in the stitching (fig. 7.12c). Notice the elongated hexagon that is formed under the center background square that is turned on point. Continue adding Bow Tie segments for seven sets. Trim off the excess triangles at each end, leaving a ¼" seam allowance (fig. 7.12d).

2. For the back, stitch two panels together. Stitch the border fabric to the sides and bottom of the panel, mitering each corner. Follow the Neck Trim schematic (fig. 7.13) to slant the outside shoulder area. Pin batting and backing together. Align the right sides of

Shoulder Trim

7

Front Trim

2 1/2

4 1/2

Figure 7.13

the pieced panel and the lining together and machine stitch around all sides, leaving a 6" opening on one side. Trim all excess batting, especially at the corners, and invert. Set the outside edges with basting stitches and slip stitch the opening closed. Machine or hand quilt to your choice.

Figure 7.14

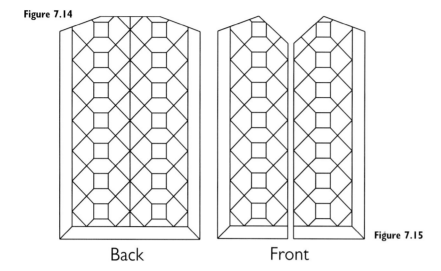

Back   Front

Figure 7.15

3. For the front, stitch the border fabric to the bottom and sides of each panel. Following the Neck Trim schematic (fig. 7.13), trim off the shoulder and front area. Pin the batting and backing together and align with right sides of decorative panel and lining facing. Sew around all sides of each panel leaving a 6" opening to invert. Trim any excess fabric, especially at corners. Invert and slip stitch opening closed. Set the outside edges with basting stitches. Machine or hand quilt each panel.

4. First draw, then cut out hood and sleeve patterns in paper (figs. 7.16 and 7.17). Place on fabric and cut out two sleeves and one hood. If using a fabric that frays, line each of these pieces.

5. Connection: With a large needle and yarn, connect the jacket, sleeves, and hood with a crossover buttonhole stitch. First, go in one side and cross over to the opposite side.

Figure 7.16

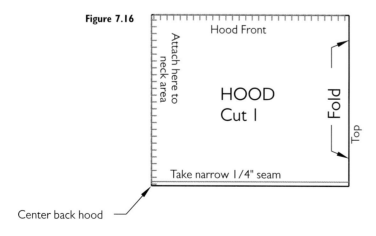

Center back hood

Begin on the bottom sides of the jacket, pinning the sleeve in place for the back and front area. Hide any loose yarns inside the lining as you run out of thread. After sides and sleeves are joined, buttonhole the top of the sleeve, continuing across the shoulder seam. Pin the midpoint of the hood in place and attach with more buttonhole stitches. Trim any extra areas such as base of jacket, sleeve ends, or front edges with more buttonhole yarn stitches. Sew five decorative buttons in the triangle area on the front panel. Make crocheted loops out of remaining yarn.

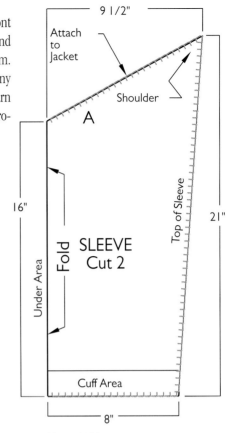

Figure 7.17

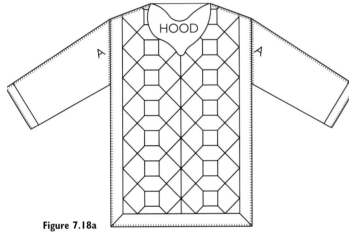

Figure 7.18a

Back

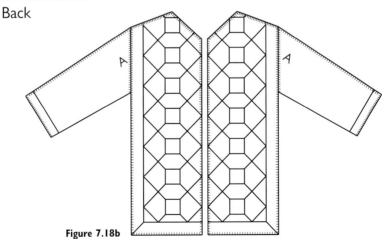

Figure 7.18b

Front

PROJECT: QUILTER'S TOTE-ALL

It just does not get any easier to make than this! And then, how great to carry a wealth of goodies, from class supplies to Christmas presents. Make this Quilter's Tote-All in several colors as special gifts for your quilting friends. This idea was passed on to me by Eleanor Bryant from New Bern, North Carolina.

Materials

1½ yards of print fabric

Two pieces of 15" elastic, ¾" wide

One pair of hoops, 9" to 12" in diameter. (Search the craft shops for these, especially where macramé products are sold.)

Method

1. Fold over 1½" on each long side to form a 1¼" casing with a ¼" hem. Insert elastic with a large safety pin through this casing, securing 5" from each end with machine stitching. Repeat for the other side. This will create gathered sides (fig. 7.19).

2. Serge or zigzag each end covering the raw edges. Fold these edges down 1¾" and wrap over the curved edges of each hoop. Stitch on the sewing machine. The fabric will gather as you stitch. This is a bit cumbersome, but you can do it! Enjoy, and carry your finished quilt to the next guild meeting.

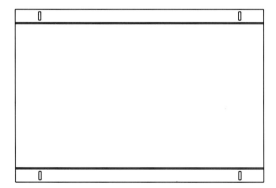

Figure 7.19

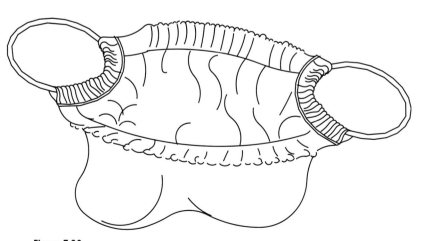

Figure 7.20

8 Making Mountains

Making mountains in patchwork has always appealed to me, perhaps because the Blue Ridge Mountains curtained in a veil of mist represent home. Maybe it's the pull of nature's colors in blue and green where I love to hike and wander down back roads. You can find up-and-down landscapes in Montana's Big Sky country or even create curved sand dunes from a coastal beach. I present to you two ideas for mountains: Seminole Skies, in small, medium, or large versions, and a Framed Mountain Fantasy collection.

PROJECT: SEMINOLE SKIES

Gather four mountain fabrics that have distinct contrast for your main fabrics. Do consider purple mountain majesty, sandy earth shades, or any prints that set mountains apart from one another. For each mountain, pick out three accent shades—twelve altogether. These will be angled strips behind each mountain that represent sunrise, sunset, or another mountain range, but they add dash and more color. The other half is the sky. Select from one of the many cloud and sky prints, considering there will be angled stitching lines. Dark sky fabrics are only successful when choosing lighter mountain shades.

A unique system of stitching sky to each mountain with accent strips in between, then cutting and re-stitching sections, results in four sets of mountains for each color.

Materials
Large
Mountain: ¾ yard of four different mountain fabrics
Sky: 3 yards
Accent strips: Cut one set for each of the four mountain fabrics
   (crosswise or straight of grain)
   A = 1¾" × 38"
   B = 1½" × 30"
   C = 1¼" × 22"

Medium
Mountain: ⅔ yard of four different mountain fabrics
Sky: 2 yards
Accent strips: Cut one set for each of the four mountain fabrics
   (crosswise or straight of grain)
   A = 1½" × 33"
   B = 1¼" × 25"
   C = 1" × 16"

Groupie Guidelines

Engage three friends to share in this project. Decide on the same size—small, medium, or large—and use the same sky fabric. Vary the array of mountain fabric, as you will keep one set of each color, give away twelve, and get twelve different sets in return. Remember that variety leads to excitement!

Small

Medium

Large (by Mary Herold)

Small

Mountain: ¼ yard of four different mountain fabrics

Sky: 1 yard

Accent strips: Cut one set for each of the four mountain fabrics
   (crosswise or straight of grain)
   A = 1¼" × 18"
   B = 1" × 14"
   C = ¾" × 9"

Step 1: Templates

Make templates using Grid Grip® (freezer paper with a continuous grid) and a ruler with 30° and 60° angles. For your desired size, follow the measurements indicated for each side of the four templates, III, II, I, and 0 (see figs. 8.1a, 8.2a, and 8.3a).

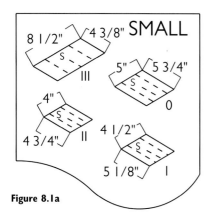

Figure 8.1a

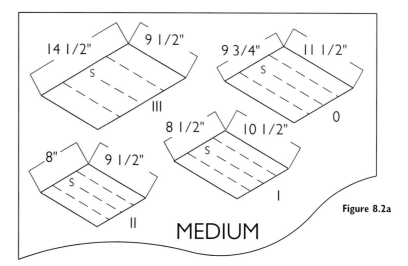

Figure 8.2a

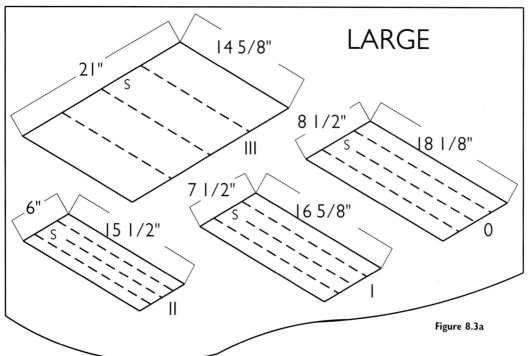

Figure 8.3a

In the corner of the Grid Grip®, place the ruler with a 30° angle aligned with the grid to include the desired length for the first long side. Trace that line indicating the length (figs. 8.1b, 8.2b, and 8.3b).

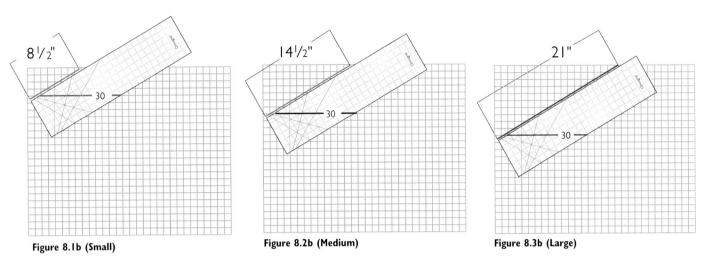

Figure 8.1b (Small)   **Figure 8.2b (Medium)**   **Figure 8.3b (Large)**

Swing ruler around to create a 120°, obtuse angle at the top, with the 30° angle line of the ruler aligned horizontally again on the grid. Indicate the adjacent side length on the paper (figs. 8.1c, 8.2c, and 8.3c).

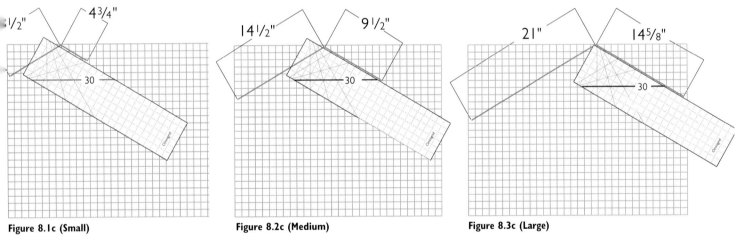

Figure 8.1c (Small)   **Figure 8.2c (Medium)**   **Figure 8.3c (Large)**

With these angles as a start, complete the other three shapes, following the measurements for II, I, and O. Indicate on each template the "S" letter that indicates the sides to be stitched together (fig. 8.4). The medium and large templates will take up more space on the Grid Grip® sheet, naturally. Enlarge gridded paper by pressing overlapped edges together.

Cut these shapes out. They are the templates for mountain and sky, with seam allowances included for all cutting and stitching.

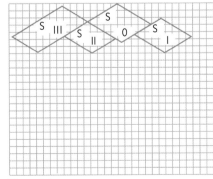

Figure 8.4

Step 2: Cutting

Mountains: Align all four mountain fabrics with right sides up, stacked on top of one another. Place templates on the right side of the fabric. The grid of the template should align with the straight of grain and crosswise of the fabric. Butt templates as close together as possible to conserve fabric, yet allow room to cut easily with a rotary cutter. Press templates in place with a dry (cotton setting) iron. Cut out each of the four templates to yield four sets of different mountain fabric. Remove the Grid Grip®, keeping each set together (fig. 8.5).

Hint

Save your templates for reuse by indicating name, size of pattern, and date used on each template. Store in an envelope.

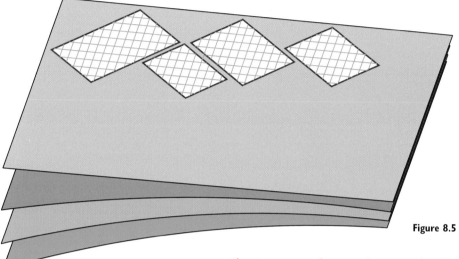

Figure 8.5

Sky: Arrange templates on sky material with excess fabric hanging loose. Press in place (fig. 8.6a). Cut around the outside of these four templates to rearrange this whole amount three more times (fig. 8.6b).

Figure 8.6a

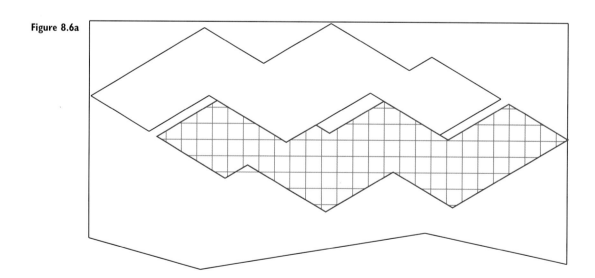

Hint

Press a small piece of Grid Grip® on each of the sets, indicating the side to be stitched ("S" marking). Keep the sets pinned together.

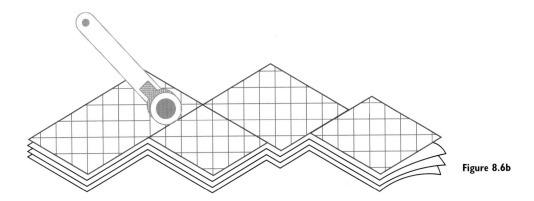

Figure 8.6b

Remember, the right side of the fabric must be up. If wrong sides of the fabric are kept together, mirror-image fabrics would be cut, creating opposite angles. Cut out the four fabric sets with four layers of sky fabric. Remove templates, marking sets III, II, I, and O plus stitching sides.

Step 3: Accent Strips

Arrange the accent strips for each mountain fabric with the longer strip, A, on the bottom and C, the shortest strip, on top. Stitch these sets together. Trim off the end on the left-hand side of each set to create a 60° angle. (see figs. 8.7a–c.) The length of these strips will be long enough to include the III, II, and I stitching.

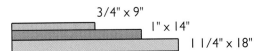

3/4" × 9"

1" × 14"

1 1/4" × 18"

Figure 8.7a

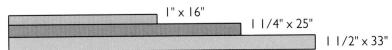

1" × 16"

1 1/4" × 25"

1 1/2" × 33"

Figure 8.7b

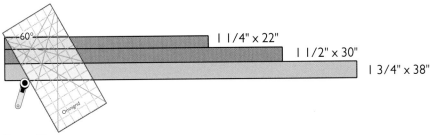

60°

1 1/4" × 22"

1 1/2" × 30"

1 3/4" × 38"

Figure 8.7c

Step 4: Stitching

Now you are ready to stitch your sets together, matching the III, II, I, and O of mountain to sky fabric, with accent strips in between. Stitch the III mountains to the III skies with the A accent strips next to the mountains. Trim off the accent strips, leaving just two strips to stitch between the next II units of mountains and skies. Continue with the I units of mountains to skies with just one remaining accent color, finishing with the O sets of mountains and skies sewn together. Note that the III sets have three accent strips, the II sets have two, the I sets have one, and the O sets just sew to each other. "Pin and peek" at each connection to ensure that all outside angles are even. There will be angled dog ears to trim. Sew with the bias edges against the feed dogs and accent strips on top. Alternate the pressing of seams on the backside: III seams press toward the skies, II seams press toward the mountains, I seams press toward the skies, and O seams press toward the mountains. This stitching results in four sets for each color of mountain fabric (fig. 8.8).

Figure 8.8

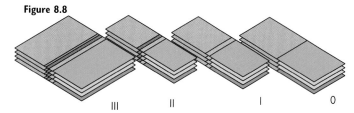

III   II   I   O

Step 5: Cut Apart

Each of the III, II, I, and O sets is now ready to be cut apart with a ruler and rotary cutter, from the long side through the pieced units. Note that there is a different measurement for each set, with a built-in excess that will be tossed away. (It's called patchwork insurance!) (See fig. 8.9.)

		III	II	I	O
		Cut Strip Widths			
Small		1 3/4"	3/4"	7/8"	1"
Med		3"	1 1/2"	1 3/4"	2"
Large		4 1/2"	1 1/4"	1 1/2"	1 3/4"

Figure 8.9

Move the off-hand that grips the ruler to be opposite these long cuts so there is no slippage. Pin the sets together—four sets for each color.

Step 6: Re-stitching

To create the mountain sections, the III, II, I, and 0 angled strips are now stitched together. Pin III and II together, and I and 0 together. Note that on the backside the seam allowances can be aligned and pinned in place. "Pin and peek" to be certain that the mountain and sky fabric seam connection is accurate on the front. Pin on the exact ¼" seam line so the fabric does not "eek" over onto the opposing color. Stitch, being careful not to stretch the bias sides. Then sew each set together, noting a "V" connection on the backside as the angled stitching lines go in opposite directions (fig. 8.10a). When all sixteen sets are sewn together, spend some time deciding on the row arrangements. It can be done with four rows of four mountains (fig. 8.10b), two rows of eight mountains (fig. 8.10c), or three rows of five mountains (losing one set) (fig. 8.10d).

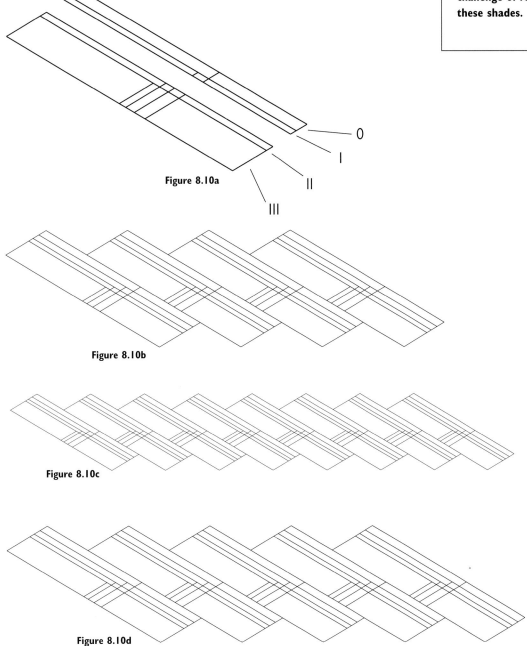

Figure 8.10a

Figure 8.10b

Figure 8.10c

Figure 8.10d

Groupie Guidelines

If you are working with three friends who are using the same sky fabric, now is the time to save four of each mountain set and give away twelve sets. You also receive a set of four from three friends, giving you a medley of sixteen different mountains. What fun to share and meet the challenge of rearranging all of these shades.

Hint

The large and medium sizes really lend themselves best to the four rows of four setting, unless you are accommodating a special room setting and desire a long wall hanging.

Sew the mountains together to create the rows with a special drop key measurement that ensures all mountain ranges will be even across. Pin the backside by measuring from the sky/mountain seam of one set to the sky/C accent seam of the next set to be attached (fig. 8.11).

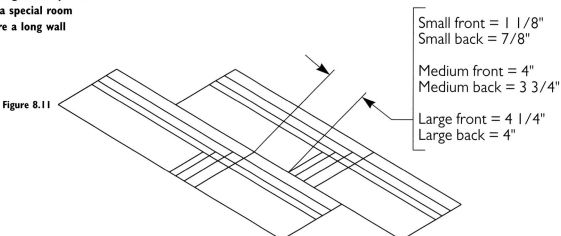

Small front = 1 1/8"
Small back = 7/8"

Medium front = 4"
Medium back = 3 3/4"

Large front = 4 1/4"
Large back = 4"

Figure 8.11

After pinning at these two points, check the front measurement also before stitching. Continue with each row by evenly sewing the ends together to form a circle. Slip a cutting mat inside this circle and cut the mountain apart right on the peak. Note how the 60° angle aligns with the stitching line to ensure a straight cut (fig. 8.12).

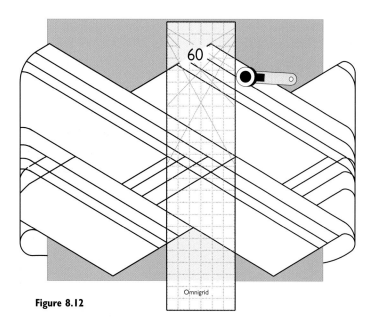

Figure 8.12

Trim excess fabric off the sky and mountain by aligning the ruler with each mountain peak (fig. 8.13). The approximate width of each row should be

Small: 3½" to 4"

Medium: 8½" to 9"

Large: 10½" to 11".

(Note: this varies according to the ¼" seams taken.)

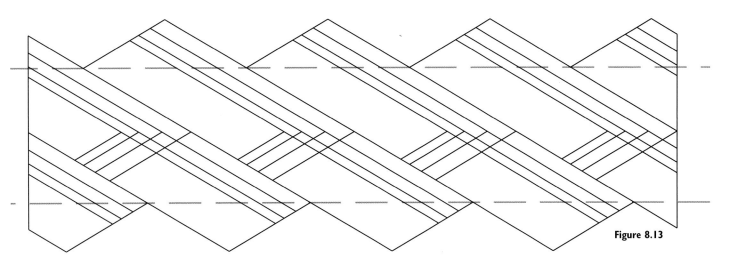

Figure 8.13

Step 7: Finishing

When the rows are stitched, add any extra mountain fabric below the pieced section and any extra sky fabric above to give each row depth. Add the same length to each row to keep the pieced sections true and not "katy wampus." The excess triangles from the large size can be used as borders when re-stitched together (fig. 8.14). It helps to measure the length and width to establish an equal division for the number of triangles. I make a template that allows me to trim the triangles into equal sections. Press any Grid Grip® templates on the front of these pieces to then add a ¼" seam allowance on all three sides. Pressing on the backside of an already pieced section will cause threads to pull apart when paper is removed.

Step 8: Quilting

Seminole piecing creates many seams, so machine quilting adapts well here. Using a walking foot and metallic blue, silver, and green threads, I quilted from side to side, starting in the center rows. I continued the same angled and curved stitching on all borders. In the medium-size wall hanging I mimicked bars of music in random fashion. Be creative; let your mind wander to all sorts of grasses, scrolls for clouds, etc.

Step 9: Binding

Refer to the quick calculation for the amount required for your chosen size of small, medium, or large. Approximate size of finished wall hanging (border addition will alter size):

Small: 18" × 44" (two rows of eight mountains)
Medium: 52" × 58" (four rows of four mountains)
Large: 58" × 67" (four rows of four mountains).

Figure 8.14

PROJECT: FRAMED MOUNTAIN FANTASY

Using Grid Grip® and a flexicurve, create soft, undulating lines on three rectangles to be framed as a triplet. This project lends itself well to hand or machine piecing.

Materials

Three Grid Grip® rectangles: 5" × 7", 7" × 9", and 7" × 14"

Fabric remnants of blue and green to represent mountains and sky

Flexicurve/pencil and indelible pen

Foam-core board (available at art supply stores). Cut

    7½" × 9½" and a colored mat with a 4½" × 6½" opening

    9½" × 11½" and a colored mat with a 6½" × 7½" opening

    9½" × 16½" and a colored mat with a 6½" × 13½" opening

Method

1. With a pencil, trace the flexicurve in a bent manner on the Grid Grip® to create soft curves. Keep the angles soft and not too severe so they will be easy to stitch. Consider rainbows, sunsets, suns, etc. Go over lines with an indelible pen once in place.

2. On the templates, code the sequence of piecing. Consider in each instance the starting and ending seams. Mark the color preference for each template. Mark any crossover clues with a notch, curved line, or dash.

3. Cut out templates. Press onto the backside of fabric, aligning grainline and leaving a full ¼" seam allowance around the outside of each template. With a rotary cutter and ruler, trim around each template, leaving a ¼" seam allowance. Transfer any crossover clues and each corner onto the fabric with a pencil or chalk.

4. Pin right sides of fabric together at corners and crossover clues; remove paper, and stitch fabric curves, aligning raw edges.

5. Cut batting same size as finished rectangle. Quilt by hand or machine. With a pencil, trace the inside opening of each mat onto the foam-core board. With a heavy-duty needle, stitch each patchwork mountainscape through the raw edges onto the foam-core board. This can even be done on the sewing machine using an open, narrow zigzag stitch. Attach the colored mat on inside top of the rectangle with masking tape.

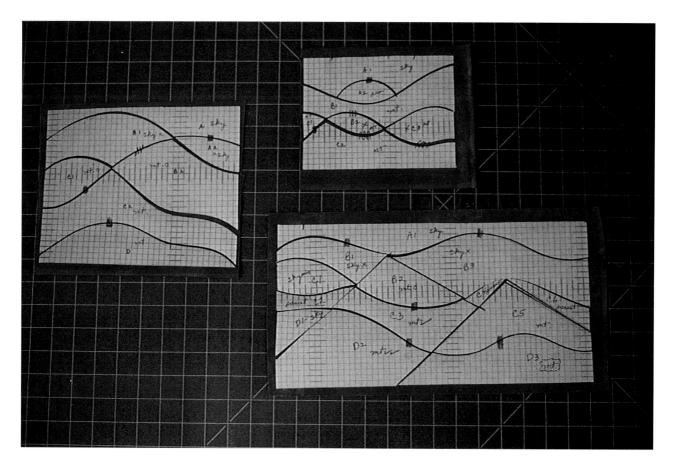

9 Questions and Answers

Yes, I receive mail. Some letters are comments, some are quilt dilemmas, some are pattern problems, but most are just the everyday questions that you and I have always pondered. These letters have become a reflection of people's achievements and a need for true quilt confession, too. So, I will attempt to give you a clear-cut response to these questions.

Do the new rotary cutter blade sharpeners really work?
If the blade is warped or has a severe nick, it will be more difficult to sharpen. However, I have increased the lifespan of a blade by using this device. Sharpeners now come in all three sizes to accommodate the blade sizes. You can also send your blades to L. P. Sharp, HC3 Box 48A, Emily, MN 56447. Be certain to save the nice plastic containers that new blades come in for handy storage or mailing.

What are those white spatulas that come in book promotion packages?
They can easily become patchwork earrings! It is really a hera. This is a narrow, sharp-curved edge that fits nicely in your hand to draw an indention on the fabric. It can be used as a quilting guide or a cutting line, but good light is essential to detect this line.

How do you collect a good fabric stash? Where do you store fabric? How much do you buy of a "don't know where it will go" fabric?
I have developed the ABC's of fabric — a dictionary of fabric designs. If you make it your goal to collect at least a yard of each of these, your quilts will take on new character. See Chapter 2, Focus on Fabric. I used to store my fabric on an inside wall of my studio. As the years have gone by, light has caused a faded ridge on the outside fold of each fabric. Now I store it in an enclosed area. Moral of this story: cover your fabric. I usually buy a yard of questionable fabric but always mark where and when I bought it so I know where to get more if I need it.

How many stitches per inch do you quilt? Is it necessary for the same size to be on the back of the quilt?
This question always worries me! Do you think our tombstones will say, "And she made twelve stitches per inch"? There are many factors involved in this answer. Yes, we are all anxious to have close, even stitches for our connection, but what about the size of your hands, the thickness of the batting, the time of the month, the size of the needle, the style of the quilt, the kind of fabric, the backing material, and the kind of quilting thread? I make anywhere from eight to twelve stitches per inch, depending on these factors. Some days the needle just flows; other days I feel very awkward. When I started quilting in a hoop for my full-sized quilts, I had to learn an entirely new method of quilting. For this method I use an indented thimble and always have the needle coming toward me for this up and down motion. As my top hand holds the needle, my thumb acts as a tension con-

troller feeling just a hint of the needle poking through on top each time. The underhand feels the needle each time as I rock up and down. For my lap quilting without a hoop, I have discovered that I hold the needle parallel to my body so that my off-hand feeds the layered fabrics to the needle. The goal is to have the stitches on the backside the same, but that rarely happens, especially through thick intersections. Who can look at the front and back at the same time anyway?

Please tell me more about using gridded freezer paper in quiltmaking.
The day the light bulb of creativity "clicked" about freezer paper, many new doors opened for me. I envisioned a continuous quarter-inch grid printed on freezer paper so I would have a graph pad, template, and sewing guide in one product. I am happy to feature these ideas in *Patchwork Potpourri*. Grid Grip® results in proper grainlines on the outside of blocks and quilts. Long bias quilt edges mean unstable raw edges with a lot of give on the perimeter of a quilt.

Is there a simple way to reduce the size of a regular quilt pattern to a small-sized pattern?
To change the size of any quilt pattern, you must determine the quilt category first. Is it a four patch, a nine patch, etc.? Today, we can often determine the templates by using our calculator. The most visible way is to draw the actual finished size of the block, isolate the number of repeat sections, and add a quarter-inch seam allowance around all sides to become templates, plus include the grainline. It does take some effort, but it's well worth the drafting experience if it encourages you to learn more about patchwork. A copy machine will not reduce or enlarge a template accurately if the template has seam allowances included, since the seam allowances need to stay at a quarter-inch.

What prompted you to become a quilter?
I had an opportunity to do some television work in New Orleans for a series called "Sewing Is Fun." The creator of that show put me in touch with some men's tie fabrics, fresh from the factory. After months of trial and error, we determined that these fabrics were best used in quilted evening bags. They did not come to life until the batting was inserted. Then the stitches created wonderful shadows on the surface. I sold these bags in the French Quarter under the label "Cajun Quilters." That launched my quilting career! Now think back on your own beginnings.

Are you in a quilt group?
Yes, I am a member of four active groups in our area, but because of my teaching travels and store obligations, I cannot attend all the meetings. That is a sincere regret of mine, since I get so stimulated when I can be with fellow quilters.

How do you feel about judged quilt shows?
Having judged many quilt shows, I find myself in somewhat of a dilemma with this answer. Every person should have a ribbon for just completing a quilt, but that would not give us the criteria we need to excel. It's like giving As and Bs in a classroom. We all need goals and inspiration to improve, and ribbons do just that. People need to enter their quilts in more than one contest, since judges can be fickle. I sometimes ask myself, "What's in a ribbon, anyway?" The answer always jumps out when I get one myself. It's a

great feeling to be chosen, to know you have been judged against your peers. Even the critiques given by judges allow you to improve and give you new ideas for more quilts.

How do you feel about machine piecing and quilting?

I look at the sewing machine as an extension of my fingers. If great-grandmother had had one, she would have used it. Many did not have that opportunity. I believe the stigma of "It's not a quilt unless it's all made by hand" is fading away. Yes, there is contentment in hand piecing, and I have been known to do that; but we are progressing in our field, just like all avenues of craft today. So I not only machine piece, but I machine quilt. I try to machine quilt in a way that does not emulate what can so beautifully be done by hand. I think of the needle as my pencil or pen and sometimes write words—I try to create "chicken scratch" symbols that can be given names such as "EKG," "lazy eights," or "loitering." I work with the feed dogs up using my walking foot, or there is the option of dropping the feed dogs for the meandering process. It takes practice and concentration. Sometimes hand quilting can act as a basting preparation for my machine quilting. Combining both elements, hand and machine quilting, can add an interesting dimension.

Do you wash all your fabrics for a quilt?

Most of the time. If it is for a wall hanging or has a special finish, I sometimes test a square in a glass of water in the microwave. If it fades, then I will prewash it using ProRetayne®.

How do you find time to do it all?

I don't. Some things just slip behind in order of priority. Anyone who is a professional in this field is very focused and committed to her work. It does mean some sacrifice—usually in friends and entertaining. It takes an understanding husband and family, that's for sure. I do run around town with yellow stickers on my blouse telling me what I forgot to do each day!

What is your favorite quilt?

That's easy. It's the first white-on-white sampler quilt I ever taught. Every once in a while I get it out and put a few more stitches on it. It represents a lot of learning, but it also was the springboard for a lifetime of teaching.

What do you consider your best quilt tip?

This question also deals with my greatest quilt aggravation—bias, stretched sides on a quilt top. I see this prevalent on old and currently made tops. Sometimes quick cutting techniques leave bias edges, ignoring the importance of stable edges for the settings of finished tops. These edges, when they occur, need to be stabilized with additional borders. The edges of a quilt top can also be stretched or distorted when many of the fabrics are cut on the crosswise grain of the fabric. So don't just pick up a length of border and sew it onto a finished quilt top. Measure twice and then cut! Take a measurement on opposite sides, both the length and width of the top. Have the top on a flat surface in line with the center of the overall top. If the edges are distorted, release or take in seams to square up the surface, ensuring that these perimeter sides are close to the center measurements. Cut borders according to this measurement plus ½" for seam allowance. Pinch and find mid-

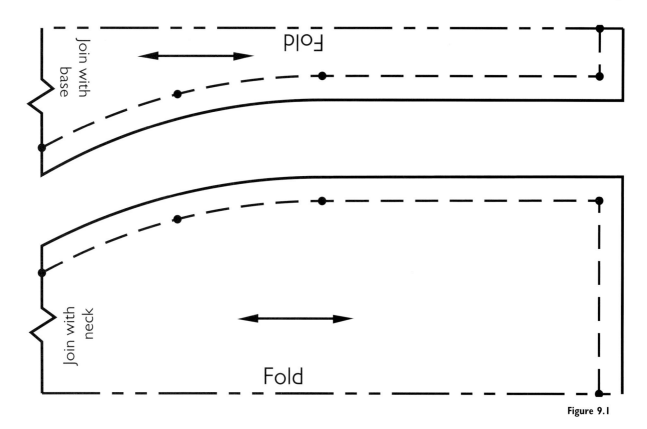

Figure 9.1

points of borders and quilt edges; align these together, pin in place, and stitch. If easing and "fudging" has to occur, pin on the backside of the borders so the quilt top is against the feed dogs when sewing. If the corners are to be mitered, sew only to the ¼" end and backstitch.

How do you get your inspiration for quilt ideas?
I work at being creative. It means being very observant, always being stimulated by stories related in class, books I read, ads I see on television, bank logos, bathroom tile, wallpaper patterns, art in museums, and quilts made yesterday as well as the modern quilts of today. All of these visual notions come together to activate the mind and hands. Many things I do require planning for the future—writing a book, creating content for thirty-minute quilting programs, or traveling—so I am always thinking ahead. That doesn't mean I don't enjoy quilting on something today. Keep a notebook of "I wanna make." It's only natural to schedule the next project as we complete one.

What can you do with the cloth bags from Seagrams Gold Label liquid refreshment? Can you suggest a quilt pattern?
After pondering these bags for months, I recalled a simple tesselated bottle design that would be most appropriate, using a medley of scrap fabrics, cut according to the templates shown (fig. 9.1), with the bottles arranged top end to bottom end, side by side. The important step here is to prewash all of the brushed cotton bags, since they really fade. Many washings will finally stabilize the purple color.

— Georgia Bonesteel

Series 900 of Lap Quilting

INDEX OF PROGRAM TITLES AND TECHNIQUES

Resources

The *Lap Quilting* 900 series was produced by the University of North Carolina Center for Public Television. To secure VHF tapes for this series, in PAL international form also, contact the North Carolina Center for Public Television, PO Box 14900, Research Triangle Park, NC 27709-4900, or phone 1-800-906-5050. Consider buying the entire series at a bulk rate for your quilt guild.

The following companies have given underwriting support for series 900 of *Lap Quilting*. They believe in our quiltmaking and consider their money invested in a good cause—learning for a lifetime.

Omnigrid, Inc., LQ
c/o Randal Schafer
1560 Port Drive
Burlington, WA 98233

VIP Fabrics, LQ
c/o Susan Neill
1412 Broadway
New York, NY 10018

Leisure Arts, LQ
c/o Thomas Carlisle
5701 Ranch Drive
Little Rock, AR 72212

Bernina of America, LQ
c/o Martin Favre
3500 Thayer Court
Aurora, IL 60504-6182

Program 901:
Round and Round We Go
Creative Curves, LQ
Virginia A. Walton
3825 Camino Capistrano, NE
Albuquerque, NM 87111

Timeless Treasures, LQ
Nancy Johnson-Srobro
Bonesteel Quilt Corner
150 White Street
Hendersonville, NC 28739

Madame Gadea, LQ
11 Rue Des Bouteilles
13100 Aix en Provence, France

L. P. Sharp, LQ (rotary cutter blades)
HC3 Box 48A
Emily, MN 56447

Program 902: Focus on Fabric
VIP Fabrics, LQ
c/o Susan Neill
1412 Broadway
New York, NY 10018

North Carolina State University, LQ
College of Textiles
Dept. of Textiles
c/o R. Alan Donaldson
Box 8301
Raleigh, NC 27695

Program 903: Design Details
The Dairy Barn, LQ
c/o Jeanne A. Donado
PO Box 747
Athens, OH 45701

Encyclopedia of Pieced Quilt Patterns
by Barbara Brackman
Encyclopedia of Appliqué
by Barbara Brackman
Bonesteel Quilt Corner
150 White Street
Hendersonville, NC 28739

Feedsack Club
c/o Jane Clark Stapel
PO Box 4168
Pittsburgh, PA 15202

Marge Edie, *Bargello Quilts*, LQ
That Patchwork Place Publishers
200 Crestwood Drive
Clemson, SC 29631

Program 904: Viva La France I
Souleiado, LQ
c/o Christiane Demery
39 Rue Proudhon
13150 Tarascon, France

Program 905: Viva La France II
Quilt Expo V, LQ
c/o American International Quilt Association
7660 Woodway Dr., Suite 550
Houston, TX 77063

Les Nouvelles du Patchwork, LQ
BP 40 75261 Paris
Cedex 06 France

Ruching Guides by Anita Shackelford
1539 Fairview Ave.
Bucyrus, OH 44820

Program 906:
Spring Forth with Flowers
Firm Foundations
c/o Jane Hall, LQ
200 Transylvania Avenue
Raleigh, NC 27609

The Foundation Piecer
Zippy Designs Publishing, LQ
RFD 1, Box 187M
Newport, VA 24128

Faces and Places
C & T Publishers
Charlotte Warr Andersen, LQ
5740 Wilderland Lane
Salt Lake City, UT 84118

Program 907:
Summertime Stitches
The Earth Quilt
c/o Norma Bradley
16 Albemarle Rd.
Asheville, NC 28801

Show and Tell, II
by Don Tyler
Bonesteel Quilt Corner
150 White Street
Hendersonville, NC 28739

Program 908: Fall into Step
Freedom Escape, LQ
Attn. Ben Wax
530 Upper Flat Creek Rd.
Weaverville, NC 28787

The Stencil Co., LQ
28 Castlewood Drive
Cheektowaga, NY 14227

Program 909:
Wintertime Wonders/Garments Galore
Manneque Productions, LQ
c/o Mary Bousfield
PO Box 2415
Menlo Park, CA 94026

American Quilters' Society, LQ
c/o Bonnie Browning
PO Box 3290
Paducah, KY 42002

Herbal Moth Repellent, LQ
RR 2, Box 128
Saegertown, PA 16433

Program 910: Button, Button,
Who's Got the Button?
Warther Museum, LQ
c/o David Warther
331 Karl Ave.
Dover, OH 44622

National Button Society, LQ
c/o Lois Pool
2733 Juno Place
Akron, OH 44333

Program 911:
Quilts, Here, There and Everywhere
Kutztown Pennsylvania German Festival
c/o Barbara Held, LQ
PO Box 306
Kutztown, PA 19530

The People's Place Museum, LQ
c/o Rachel T. Pellman
76 Greenfield Rd.
Lancaster, PA 17602

Susan Baker, Antique Button Vendor, LQ
123 Encino Blanco
San Antonio, TX 78232

Program 912: Seminole Skies I
Coming Home (Division of Lands' End), LQ
c/o Anna Schryver, PR Specialist
5 Land's End Lane
Dodgeville, WI 53595

Program 913: Seminole Skies II
Le Rouvray, LQ
c/o Diane de Obaldia
1 Rue Rederic Sauton
75005 Paris, France

Index